CN00662967

The
DEER STALKER'S
BEDSIDE BOOK

THE
DEER STALKER'S
BEDSIDE BOOK

Charles Smith-Jones

Illustrations by Keith Sykes

Quiller

For Sara, David and James

Copyright © 2015 Charles Smith-Jones
Illustrations copyright © 2015 Keith Sykes

First published in the UK in 2015
by Quiller, an imprint of Quiller Publishing Ltd

British Library Cataloguing-in-Publication Data
A catalogue record for this book is available from the British Library

ISBN 978 1 84689 206 6

The right of Charles Smith-Jones to be identified as the author of this work
has been asserted in accordance with the Copyright, Design and Patent Act 1988.
The information in this book is true and complete to the best of our knowledge.
All recommendations are made without any guarantee on the part of the
Publisher, who also disclaims any liability incurred in connection
with the use of this data or specific details.

All rights reserved. No part of this book may be reproduced or transmitted in
any form or by any means, electronic or mechanical including photocopying,
recording or by any information storage and retrieval system,
without permission from the Publisher in writing.

Design by Arabella Ainslie
Edited by Kirsty Ennever

Illustrations by Keith Sykes
Cover painting by Ben Hoskyns

Printed in Malta

Quiller
An imprint of Quiller Publishing Ltd
Wykey House, Wykey, Shrewsbury, SY4 1JA
Tel: 01939 261616 Fax: 01939 261606
E-mail: info@quillerbooks.com
Website: www.quillerpublishing.com

CONTENTS

Anecdotes, Curiosities,

Tall Tales and Yarns appear throughout

FOREWORD

I first met Charles Smith-Jones when I measured one of his roe heads on behalf of the Game Conservancy in the very early 1980s (it was a beautiful, lyre-shaped Salisbury Plain head), a time when deer stalking was still very much in its infancy compared to the large following that it has today. Since then I have followed his developing stalking career through articles in *Shooting Times* and *Deer* magazines with great interest and enjoyment. His pioneering book on muntjac was a milestone in our understanding of this species, which has been his special interest.

Charles has never lost sight of his enthusiasm for deer and their deep fascination for him is reflected among the pages of this book. I am delighted that in this volume he has found a wider outlet for the mass of experiences, facts and trivia that he has accumulated over the years.

Writing about actual stalking occurrences and observations, creating sporting stories and researching bits of stalking lore from a mass of sporting literature to make an anthology both interesting and informative needs all-out enthusiasm for the deer themselves and some considerable practical experience of stalking. In presenting this *Bedside Book*, Charles Smith-Jones has done a masterly job. Reaching from your pillow you have the choice of answers to many frequently asked questions or lively stalking reminiscences and stories, short or less so.

I wish I had written it myself!

Richard Prior

INTRODUCTION

Deer were, and still are, few and far between where I grew up on the North Wales coast but I distinctly remember seeing my first wild ones (they were a group of fallow does) when out beating on my father's shoot aged about eight. It was not until much later on that I became actively involved in stalking but from the moment I grassed my first roebuck my interest in them grew rapidly. I suspect that it is true of any hunter that the more you get to know your quarry, the more you learn to respect it and want to know more of its ways, and paradoxically this tends to make you more successful in your pursuit.

In addition to actual stalking and management, I quickly found that I became hooked on deer as an interest in their own right. They grow on you; the more you think you know, the more you come to realise that there is so much still to learn. I count myself truly privileged that my second career after more than thirty years in uniform finds me sharing this love of all things deer, along with the issues that surround them, with a new generation of countrymen and women at Sparsholt College in Hampshire.

It has been tremendous fun assembling this collection of stories, advice, facts and trivia. Although the book is primarily concerned with stalking here in the UK, I have occasionally strayed off track, but do hope that you'll forgive me. I very much doubt, for instance, that any deer was ever shot with the improbable (but very real) Puckle Gun, but I couldn't resist sharing a description of it anyway.

Before you read on, you ought to be aware that I have included one outrageously untrue deer 'fact' which is hidden somewhere within the text. If you would rather be forewarned you can turn to the back page now to find out what it is; if not, I'm sure that you'll enjoy the challenge of looking out for it.

Whatever your interest in deer, I do hope that you find this book interesting, entertaining and maybe even instructive. Finally, may I close with a suggestion: if you, too, appreciate deer and care for their welfare, why not consider joining the British Deer Society and getting involved?

Deer have provided me with a huge amount of pleasure over the years, and I've found that it is a great way of giving something back.

ACKNOWLEDGEMENTS

There are always several people who need to be thanked whenever a book is completed. In no particular order, they include Kate Gatacre of *Sporting Gun* for putting the idea into my head in the first place, and Andrew Johnston at Quiller for his encouragement and enthusiasm for the project, along with his editorial and design wizards Kirsty Ennever and Arabella Ainslie, who have so patiently and expertly sorted a very mixed bag of raw material into a volume of which to be proud. Special thanks go to Alastair Balmain (formerly of *Shooting Times*), and Graham Downing, editor of *Deer*, for generously allowing me to use some material previously published in their magazines. I am also deeply grateful that Richard Prior, whose work I have admired since my earliest stalking days, so kindly agreed to provide the Foreword.

I would like to record my appreciation to those experts in their specific fields who have advised me along the way and single out three in particular: John Thornley, for his help regarding legal aspects, and Peter Green and Alastair Ward, the Veterinary and Scientific Advisors respectively to the British Deer Society. I am especially indebted to Norma Chapman, for looking over the snippets of deer biology and trivia with a critical eye, and for ensuring that I have stayed on the straight and narrow. I would also like to take this opportunity to record my very special gratitude to that stalwart supporter of BDS training, Alex Jagger, who more than anyone else encouraged me to progress from deer stalker to manager. Without his inspiration, support and mentorship, I very much doubt that I (like so many others who have also benefited from his experience and selfless guidance over the years) would have moved forwards in my association with deer. Thank you, Alex.

Finally, I must pay tribute to my wife, Sara, for her unceasing encouragement and honest criticism as this book took shape. I couldn't have done this without her support and patience.

Charles Smith-Jones

THE DEER STALKER'S A – Z

AGEING MUNTJAC

Whilst the stages of tooth eruption in younger animals and tooth wear are useful guides to ageing a muntjac, there are a number of other pointers that can help you reach a judgement.

A muntjac fawn's spots fade at around two months of age (coincidentally, the age at which the fawn is weaned). Thereafter the face is a guide: as with all deer, a short 'Bambi' face indicates a young animal whose adult teeth have not grown through and caused the jaw to elongate. By around a year old, the animal's muzzle will have lost its short juvenile shape, appearing longer and more tapered.

Muntjac reach adult body weights very quickly and appear fully grown by the time they are about ten months old. After that it is not so easy to make an estimate of age from body shape as it can be with other deer, but look for a slight dip in the line of the back, a more muscular rump and a deeper belly in the older animal (but do not be confused by pregnant females, which might be seen at any time of the year). Age also brings caution – an older muntjac acts in a more alert and suspicious manner than a younger one.

The skull of the muntjac buck provides more clues. Male fawns start to develop pedicles at about five or six months old, and their first antlers start to develop from about three months after that. These will be rudimentary affairs with no coronet, appearing almost as mere extensions to the bone. Subsequent antlers will be rather more complex, but as with all deer cannot be used as a definitive guide to age. However, with successive antler casting the pedicles will shorten and thicken; a very old buck will not have the distinctive long pedicles of the younger animal. The antlers of old muntjac can vary between the impressive and mere stubs. Look, too, at the opening at the base of the canine tusk – that of a young buck is completely open and fully exposes the dentine within; with age, the top of the tusk will gradually close over.

AMMUNITION SIZES

Most ammunition types are designated by the size of the projectile, although the unit of measurement may vary. The 7x57 indicates a 7mm bullet, whereas the .308 refers to size as a fraction of an inch, as does the '30' in 30-06.

The suffixes can mean different things: .308 Win means simply that Winchester was the manufacturer who developed the cartridge. The '06' in 30-06 means that the cartridge originated in 1906, but the second '30' in 30-30 indicates that the cartridge was originally designed for loading with 30 grains of black powder (even though the advent of modern smokeless powder has changed this, the old designation has been retained). In yet another system, such as 7x57, the case length is 57mm. In some older cartridges, the suffix can denote the case type – for example, R for rimmed or RGS for rimless.

The shotgun bore sizes are more archaic, relating to fractions of an Imperial pound in weight – thus a 1 bore would be the width of barrel required to accommodate a spherical ball of lead weighing 1 pound, a 12 bore a lead ball weighing 1/12th of a pound, and so on. The .410 is an exception to this rule and describes the width of the barrel as a fraction of an inch.

It is vitally important to understand exactly what ammunition is suitable for use with your particular firearm, as cartridges are not interchangeable. To try to use the wrong size, even if it seems to load easily, is courting disaster.

Any time a boy is ready to learn about guns is the time he's ready, no matter how young he is, and you can't start too young to learn how to be careful.
Robert Ruark, The Old Man and the Boy

ANTLERED FEMALES

The females of any of the deer species – with one notable exception – do not normally grow antlers. However, some occasionally do so, even though this is quite rare. The condition is caused by a hormonal imbalance resulting in the production of abnormal levels of the male hormone testosterone, which stimulates the antler cycle in male deer. Female deer have been known to develop fully formed, if stunted or abnormal, antlers, which are cleaned of velvet (the furry layer that covers, protects and nourishes the delicate antler as it develops), cast and regrown in the same way that those of male deer are. More usually, however, when females grow antlers they tend to remain perpetually in velvet. Reproduction does not seem to be affected, and these animals can breed normally.

Antlered female deer have been recorded mostly amongst roe deer in the UK, although they have also been noted in sika, whitetail deer, mule deer, moose, red deer and the closely related wapiti or American elk. Very occasionally, true hermaphrodite deer with both male and female characteristics occur. These produce antlers in the usual way, but are almost invariably infertile. More often, some older female deer can develop enlarged pedicles (the bony growths on top of the skull from which antlers usually grow) but nothing more. Again, this occurrence is most commonly noted among roe deer in the UK.

The exception to the rule of females not carrying antlers is the reindeer or caribou. In this species, antlers are produced by both males and females; the two genders even have separate cycles for antler casting and regrowth. It has been suggested that this is to give the caribou cow an advantage in the leaner winter months as only they have antlers at that time, which helps them to compete for limited food supplies and to defend themselves against predators. However, the antlers of the caribou cow are relatively small compared to those of the more impressive headgear seen on the male, or bull.

ANTLERS AND HORNS

Deer are unique in being the only animals to have antlers. Normally cast and regrown annually as paired structures, antlers are produced by the males of most species with the exception of the musk and the Chinese water deer. Female reindeer also produce antlers.

Antler growth and casting is controlled by a number of hormones, the principal one being the male hormone testosterone, whose production is governed by the length of daylight hours. The growing antler is living bone: as it develops it is covered by a furry skin called velvet, which supplies it with oxygen and nutrients. At the end of the growth cycle the velvet is lost and the material within dies, rendering the antler hard and insensitive. After a few months the join between antler and skull weakens and the antlers fall off. The process of regrowth begins again almost immediately.

Horns, on the other hand, consist of a living bone projecting from the skull which never dies back and which is covered by a sheath of a tough protein called keratin, the same material found in human fingernails. Horns are grown by ruminant animals such as goats, sheep, cows and antelope. They are generally retained throughout an animal's life, and continue to grow as it matures. There is only one exception to this rule – the pronghorn antelope of North America, which sheds and regrows its horn sheath every year. This interesting animal is really neither a deer nor an antelope, although it is related to both, belonging in a distinct family of its own.

AS OTHERS SEE US

O wad some Power the giftie gie us, To see oursels as ithers see us!
Robert Burns, *To A Louse – On seeing one on a lady's bonnet at church*

It doesn't seem so long ago that the general public were quite used to the sight of sporting firearms, and every self-respecting schoolboy not only carried a penknife in his pocket but proudly sported a wicked-looking sheath knife on his belt when out hunting pirates or building a den at the weekend. Nowadays all that has changed. The country pub that invites a shooting party to bring its guns into the bar or restaurant is rare indeed, and we all know of the penalties that can apply to openly carrying a knife.

Changes in attitude in this country have been shaped by a number of factors over the past forty or fifty years. National Service once meant that a much larger proportion of the public were familiar with firearms, but the advent of domestic and international terrorism, a shift in political attitudes, deliberate misrepresentation and, let's face it, some shockingly unbalanced media reporting, have changed all that. Today, even the pigeon shooter has to take care if he doesn't want to find himself looking down the barrel of a Glock with a police helicopter hovering overhead simply because a passer-by has reported a 'man with a gun'.

It is all a question of image and how we present ourselves as sportsmen and wildlife managers. For example, it's very common to hear people talking about their shotgun or rifle as a 'weapon'. The word, however, has very negative connotations. A weapon is to most people associated with threatening or physically harming another human being. Everyday objects such as cars, bricks or bottles can very easily be misused as weapons, but of course that wasn't what they were actually designed for so that is not how they are regarded. Sporting firearms are just the same, but try telling that to a member of the public with the wrong impression, or a reporter or politician on a mission. Ex-military types can be the worst offenders in this respect, but then during their time in the Forces they were not issued with firearms for show or to shoot pheasants.

A real bugbear of mine is the 'imaginary shotgun'. I suspect that most of us have been guilty of this gesture at some time or another, most likely in our younger days: a pigeon passes overhead, and both arms are immediately raised in an almost involuntary reaction, as if to swing through it. I see this mime played out occasionally by one of my gamekeeping students, largely as an act of youthful exuberance. But I have to ask – what message does it send out to an onlooker? You are in effect saying 'I want to kill that'. It's far better, I suggest, to leave the imaginary shotgun in the imaginary cabinet where it belongs; sadly the fact that large sections of the public have been educated to regard shooters as dangerous, killing-obsessed monsters is not imaginary. I have no doubt that my students think I'm a bit of a fussy old maid, but they do get the point (and I bet they couldn't show me their imaginary shotgun certificates anyway).

Is it by chance, I wonder, that the attitude of the general public towards sporting shooting tends to be much more tolerant on the Continent? One reason for this may be the respect that is shown towards the quarry once it is dead. At the end of a formal day, the bag is laid out in a strictly observed ritual and horn calls are sounded, often a particular one for each species. Large game hunters follow a similar convention; on a recent trip to the Baltic coast, after a successful shot my guide's first act was to seek out a sprig of juniper to place in the animal's mouth as a 'last bite' to take it into the afterlife. Compare this to the sight of pheasants piled up in the spare tyre on the Land Rover bonnet, or those ridiculous – and unsubstantiated – rumours of unwanted partridges being bulldozed into the ground that have a certain currency in the UK. If you feel that a bit of ceremony is over the top, consider this: respect for the quarry has a very practical side to it, because the better game is handled, the higher is the quality of the meat that ends up on the plate.

Hunting associations on the Continent also run a number of public education programmes. I attended one in Denmark that was aimed at schoolchildren: they were encouraged to dissect ducks, act out a hunt, shoot at a deer target and finally butcher a roe, which they later enjoyed on the barbecue. Another initiative encouraged local villagers to take part in an organised pheasant shoot as spectators, and to share the proceeds at the end. Is it any wonder that those with no particular interest in shooting or hunting, will decide for themselves if presented with honest information, often rejecting the half-truths and misrepresentations of anti-fieldsports activists?

In the UK we seem to be far too defensive at times, if not downright secretive, about what we do. You might be surprised by how receptive the average walker is to a polite explanation of what is going on and why, if he should meet a stalker or a rough shooter pursuing his occupation. If there is nothing to be ashamed of, why not let people make up their own minds? The general public are, by and large, remarkably fair-minded given the chance – and the facts. And never forget that a cheerful 'good morning' and a smile can go a long way. I came very close to turning 'anti' myself once, when confronted by an arrogant, superior being on horseback who offered no apology for holding up a busy country lane whilst the hunt went through.

Of course, good news generally does not make it onto the front page in the general press. All the positive work that shooting and stalking do for the environment, all the jobs created and the huge amounts of hard cash generated for the economy usually go unreported there – but let one tawny owl be found in an illegal pole trap, or a buzzard picked up full of number six shot, and it is headline stuff. Furthermore, it is absolutely impossible to defend the indefensible.

The opponents of fieldsports are not perfect and often get things wrong themselves. I still chuckle when I think of a poster I once saw, advertising a 'garden watch' event run by a vociferously anti-shooting national animal charity that counts many cat owners among its subscribers. It pictured a cat looking out of a window, presumably into its owner's garden. The caption read: 'I saw three wrens, they're my favourite'. Make of that what you like.

The representative organisations do a magnificent job of defending the interests of fieldsports, but in the end good PR is the business of each and every one of us. We need to think about every turn of phrase, the images that we post on public access media, and how we ultimately appear to the wider public in dress, motivation and deed. Above all, we need to be open about what we do, why we enjoy doing it and why it is important for the good of the countryside that we love.

CALLING DEER

The art of calling is probably most associated with the roe deer. It is particularly effective during the rut, which starts around the last week of July and goes on into the beginning of August. A range of sounds can be made to imitate, for example, a receptive doe, one that is being hard pressed by a buck, or a kid calling for its mother. All are designed to attract a buck – or a doe with a buck in attendance – to the caller.

Calling also works for other species of deer as long as the right sounds are imitated. The most common ones used are the challenge of a dominant male, or the rattle of antlers to suggest a contest, thus attracting the interest of another deer. Muntjac can be particularly responsive to calls, often seeming to come out of little more than a sense of curiosity.

There are plenty of commercially made calls available, reproducing a wide variety of deer sounds; some skilled callers make their own, or adapt natural materials. If you want to know more, there is a lot of stalking literature that covers the subject. For calling roe, you will be hard-pressed to find a better introduction to the art than the DVD, *Roe Calling with Richard Prior and Paul Taylor*.

A few words of caution, though. Don't overdo the calling, as all you will end up doing is educating the deer. And don't expect it to work every time. It's not unusual to experience periods of great success alongside others of unexplainable failure. Beware, too, that the arrival of a large male deer answering a challenge, full of adrenaline and prepared to give battle, can be alarming to say the least. Finally, when calling does work, please don't abuse your success, particularly if you are armed with a rifle. Remember especially that any female deer that comes to your call is quite likely to have a dependent kid hidden nearby.

There is a passion for hunting something deeply implanted in the human breast. **Charles Dickens, *Oliver Twist***

CAMOUFLAGE CLOTHING
FOR DEER STALKING

Although it would be wrong to say that deer are colour blind, they certainly do not perceive colours in the same way that humans do. Importantly, they can see ultraviolet, which our eyes filter out – as a result, it is quite possible that a camouflage outfit that deceives the human eye will stand out like a beacon when viewed by a deer. You should take special care, therefore, when washing your deer-watching or stalking clothing. Most commercial washing powders contain UV brighteners and should be avoided; specialist washing compounds that do not contain them are available. Don't forget to flush the washing machine with clean water before you use it, to remove traces of any earlier household wash with normal detergents.

Whilst camouflaged clothing can certainly help to break up your outline at closer ranges, it is movement that will really give away your presence as far as the deer is concerned. It is unlikely to be able to discern shape or form at much beyond sixty or seventy metres, but it will be acutely aware of movement at many times this distance. It will also be aware of differences in colour tones, hence the importance of wearing gloves (your hands will be moving regularly when raising and lowering your binoculars), and shading your face with a broad-brimmed hat or a face veil.

Many experienced stalkers opt for a plain, moss green outfit, finding this colour to be effective throughout all seasons. An added advantage of plain green is that it is less alarming to any member of the public who you might come upon. Otherwise it is not really important what you decide to wear, as long as it is drab and inconspicuous. It should also, of course, be quiet when moving through close cover, comfortable, and of a weight appropriate to the time of year.

Tales from Glen Garron

A Stalker's Revenge

**Revenge, they say, is a dish best served cold
– or occasionally hot and bothered**

Some people mistakenly judged Willie Cameron, head stalker on the Glen Garron estate, to be a soft man, but looks can be deceptive. Standing some five feet and seven inches tall, and with the build of a committed trencherman, Willie was anything but soft. The more perceptive noted the determined blue eyes and weather-beaten features of a true hill-man, one who had in fact spent the past forty years walking moor and mountain for six days a week (the Sabbath, of course, was sacred) in pursuit of the wild red deer, the wily grouse and the occasional fox foolish enough to settle in the fifteen thousand acres that was Willie's domain. A five o'clock start, on a day during which he would cover many miles and climb thousands of feet, often returning with a fourteen-stone stag dragging behind him, was bread and butter to him.

Willie's son, Archie, took after his father in stamina if not in looks. At over six feet tall, he had the wiry frame of a fell runner and indeed for the past eight years had been the virtually uncontested Hill Race Champion at the annual Glen Garron Gathering. Like his father, the mountains of the

Highlands were in his blood and Willie looked forward proudly to the day when Archie would take over from him and carry on a family tradition that went back for generations.

Much as Willie loved his job and had a deep and abiding respect for his laird, the Colonel – the two had played together as boys – there was one week every year that he dreaded, and that week was now upon him. This last week in September was always reserved for the Colonel's brother-in-law, an aristocratic Continental gentleman whom the Colonel's sister had married in what was locally considered a rare flash of poor judgement. The Count, as he insisted on being known, had been born to privilege and entertained no illusions as to his own standing in the world. For him, only the best was barely good enough: he expected deference, expressed no thanks and worst of all, in Willie's view, had never been known to offer gift or tip after the most strenuous efforts had been made to ensure his success on the hill. And today, once again, Willie had to take him out for a stag.

The first morning dawned bright and cloudless as the stalkers, guests and hosts gathered in front of the Lodge. The day promised to be a hot one. The Count stepped forward and peered disdainfully down his nose at Willie. 'Today', he announced, 'we are to shoot a Royal, yes?'

Willie removed his cap and scratched his head. He had several such deer on his ground, all bearing the coveted twelve points to their antlers, but he chose to look thoughtful. 'Well, we'll do our best for ye' – he omitted the 'sir' quite deliberately – 'but ye know that there's nae guaranteeing...'

He got no further. The Count gripped his shoulder, stared him in the eye and quietly repeated 'a Royal'. It was a statement, not a question. The Colonel, a man of impeccable manners who respected Willie as deeply as this was returned, looked on aghast. 'Look, Gustav, I know that Willie will do his best for you. He's the best stalker in this neck of the woods and if anyone can find you a good beast, he can.'

The Count ignored him. Punctuating each word with a prod of his finger into Willie's chest, he repeated 'Today' (poke) 'we' (poke) 'shoot' (poke) 'a' (poke) 'Royal'. He concluded with a double poke, turned on his heel, and marched towards the waiting Land Rover.

A horrified Colonel broke the silence. 'Willie, I'm sorry. But, just for me, look after him will you?'

Willie exhaled carefully, then smiled and nodded. 'Aye, for ye, that I shall.' The Colonel breathed a sigh of relief; he had seen Willie's temper at work before, on the rare occasions that it had been provoked. 'I think that my wee Archie should take him oot, though. He's got some rare beasts on his beat.' Agreement was readily given.

Archie was summoned and a short conference took place between father and son before the latter, with a friendly smile, joined the Count in the Land Rover. The party drove off up the gravel drive, and the Colonel and his wife retired into the Lodge.

Later that morning, the two of them were out walking when Lady Mary pointed towards the distant ridgeline. 'Look, darling, isn't that our stalkers?' The Colonel lifted his ancient binoculars. Up on the hill was the familiar figure of Archie striding easily through the heather, rifle slip and satchel over his back, with the Count, unencumbered but clearly some way behind, in his wake. As they watched, Archie crouched down and beckoned the Count forward. Looking for what they had seen, the Colonel picked up a large stag with a parcel of fifteen hinds some three hundred yards ahead of them. 'Oh dear God,' he groaned, 'not Caesar, don't let him have Caesar.'

Caesar was probably the finest stag seen at Glen Garron in living memory, a huge-bodied animal who this year had produced a breathtaking set of evenly balanced antlers with no less than sixteen points to them. The Colonel and Willie had agreed that he was to be left this year; now it looked as though, of all people, the Count was to shoot him.

The pair watched as the drama unfolded. Archie and the Count crawled forwards to a hummock in the heather, the rifle was set onto its bipod and Archie moved to one side to allow the Count to get behind it. Before he could settle, though, something pale fluttered over his head and the deer, alerted, stared for a moment and then quickly fled the scene. 'Saved by a bird!' the Colonel thought, as he breathed out in relief, muttering his thanks to a watching deity. Lady Mary, watching through her own, more modern glasses, cocked her head, understood, smiled quietly but held her peace.

It was late when the Land Rover returned to the Lodge that evening. The passenger door opened and a dishevelled, dirty and sweat-streaked Count almost fell out of it. The Colonel was there to greet him. He was surprised to see that the open back of the vehicle did not contain a carcase. 'No luck, Gustav?' he asked. All he got in return was a grunt as the Count staggered – the Colonel noted that he was also limping badly – towards the house. Archie, looking as fresh as he had that morning, exchanged a few polite words with his laird before he, too, returned to his family home.

Willie was waiting when his son walked through the door. 'Ye did as I said then?'

'Aye, Dad, I walked the legs off yon furrin scunner. There's only one person has the right to speak to you like that, and she's in the kitchen.'

Willie frowned. 'But ye didnae find the man a beast? Hell, boy, but ye must be losing your touch.'

'Aye, Dad', Archie replied. 'So I must. We stalked four good stags, and not one of them stood for a shot.' At this the two burst out laughing as Willie fetched the malt, and they settled down, still chortling, to await their dinner.

The next week saw Archie's birthday and he was surprised to receive, in addition to his usual gift from the Lodge, a small package addressed to him in Lady Mary's handwriting. Inside it were half a dozen pure white squares of finest Irish linen. Puzzled, Archie unfolded the note that accompanied them:

> *Dearest Archie,* it read, *I couldn't help but notice how grubby your handkerchief was the other day on the hill. I hope that these are useful, but do please try to keep one clean for next year. With warmest regards and gratitude, M.*

CANINE TEETH

Whilst canine teeth are usually present in the lower jaws of most deer, it is the presence of upper canines or 'tusks' in the upper jaw which often cause surprise and suggest, wrongly, that such deer are habitual meat-eaters. Deer have digestive systems designed for the processing of vegetable matter. Their specially adapted digestive tracts contain micro-organisms which are specifically capable of destroying the cellulose walls of plants, a process further assisted by the act of rumination – the regurgitation of food matter for further chewing and breaking down prior to being swallowed again. Meat, therefore, is not a food source normally sought by deer.

In Britain, it is male muntjac and Chinese water deer (CWD) that have the most visible upper canines, although females also carry far less obvious ones. Of the other species, smaller tusks can be found on the upper jaws of sika and red deer. In the latter they are often referred to as 'tushes', and are especially prized as *grandeln* by some Continental hunters who make them into items of jewellery. The upper canine is normally absent in fallow and roe deer, although they may still be found very occasionally.

Canine-type teeth evolved as weapons in a wide range of primitive animals; some retained them as they evolved, while they regressed in others. As far as deer are concerned, the more complex their antlers are, the more evolved the species is likely to be. Some more primitive deer species have never even developed antlers at all, instead retaining the upper canines as their sole combat weapon. The CWD and musk deer are prime examples. Others, such as the muntjac, carry simple antlers but have retained a significant canine tusk. These tusks are of great importance to the male deer both for self-defence and for fighting with rival males. Animals that break one or both tusks frequently suffer a loss of dominance, and subsequently their breeding success diminishes.

It would be wrong to say that, whilst deer are herbivores, they never eat meat. Although many species are known to chew old bones or antlers regularly, red deer in particular have been recorded as killing the chicks of the Manx shearwater on the island of Rhum by biting off and swallowing their heads. There have also been reports of stags eating grouse chicks, rabbits killed in snares, and even swallowing ducklings in parks. Such behaviour is probably related to a craving for calcium amongst male deer as they grow new antlers, and is certainly not to be regarded as a regular source of nutrition.

Sonic Devices

These days it is easy to obtain sonic devices, usually operating on pitches only audible to animal ears, which the makers claim will deter a variety of animals such as cats, foxes, rodents or deer from entering your garden or other places where they are not welcome. Some of these gadgets, it must be said, seem to be quite effective, although different animals can be more sensitive to specific frequencies.

Not so long ago, though, such gizmos were not readily available in the UK. A friend, recently returned from the USA, presented me with an early model he had picked up as a curiosity in a shooting store. It was called the 'Animal Lover' and was designed to be mounted on your car to prevent animals from running onto the road in front of it. Wired to the battery, the device was only activated when the vehicle was running.

I must admit that, while sceptical, I was intrigued by the concept and decided to test it. I attached it to the front bumper of my old Land Rover and, as an added refinement, fitted an on/off switch so that I could activate it when I wanted to from the dashboard.

The next morning I toured my stalking grounds where we never shot from, or near, vehicles, and as a result the deer were quite relaxed in their presence. Seeing a roe doe with two kids, I stopped the Land Rover and thought I'd see what effect the Animal Lover had. I flipped the switch; the kids ignored me completely, and their mother continued to stare in my direction, chewing occasionally on a mouthful of freshly cropped herbage, showing no concern.

Undeterred, I tried it again on several more animals with no effect whatsoever. Discounting the gadget as a useless gimmick and deciding to get rid of it, I drove home to find the family cat – a large, battle-scarred tom, which brought home fully grown rabbits to play with and which was given a wide berth by the local dogs – sleeping peacefully on our doorstep. Idly I switched on the Animal Lover, with unexpected results: the cat went from deep slumber to three feet off the ground in one movement and fled at enormous speed. It was not seen again for several days.

I removed the device and decided to keep quiet.

CARCASE STORAGE

For the stalker who does not shoot enough animals to warrant the installation of full-blown game storage facilities, storing a carcase effectively can be a real problem. This is especially so during the summer months when the heat and ever-present flies will conspire to ruin the venison long before it reaches the deep freeze.

At the most basic level, you need to hang the carcase in a cool, dry place, out of casual view; a challenge if you live in a residential area and the garage is your only option. You can opt for a semi-permanent structure, such as a game larder with a washable floor and sides and sufficient ventilation to keep the carcase well aired. Alternatively, it is possible to purchase net or muslin covers which will keep the flies off the deer and can be put through the washing machine after use. Better yet, consider purchasing a Roe Safe, an ingenious cover design that folds flat when not in use but pops up to produce a semi-rigid, oval hanging net, big enough to contain a couple of roe or even a large fallow.

One of the key principles in producing quality venison is to cool the carcase quickly, so why not obtain a chiller cabinet? Although purpose-made game fridges are available commercially for those who deal regularly with larger numbers of carcases, it may be possible to acquire a surplus drink cooler cabinet from a shop or petrol station undergoing a refit. A six-foot high model can accommodate two roe comfortably. Simply fit a hanging rail, but keep the shelves somewhere and you will then have a versatile extra fridge for Christmas or parties – more than enough reason to justify the garage space to the rest of your household!

CHOOSING THE RIGHT BULLET

We ask a great deal of the bullets that we use for stalking. They have to withstand tremendous pressures on firing, yet still maintain their shape and fly consistently and accurately towards the target. When they reach it, they must then perform equally consistently and expand predictably, despite meeting varying resistances from skin, bone and whatever else stands in the way, to transmit maximum energy and achieve a clean and effective result. Modern hunting bullets are a testament to some truly exacting design and manufacturing processes. Whilst the law lays down no requirements of the bullets used for vermin and pest control, it is more specific when it comes down to the shooting of deer. Bullets must be designed to expand in a predictable manner on striking the target to ensure that the deer is killed as swiftly and humanely as possible. Bullets that do not expand properly can pass straight through their target without deforming correctly, transmitting much less terminal energy and potentially delivering a non-lethal wound even if they strike what should be a critical organ.

The matter of choice can be confused by a wide array of trade names. Try to look past these and see what a particular cartridge is actually designed to do. Without going into the details of bullet construction, as a general rule you should avoid those described as 'full metal jacket', 'varmint', 'rapid expansion' or 'slow expansion', or indeed those designated as 'for large or dangerous game'. What you need is a bullet that is designed and constructed appropriately for use on medium game.

Take special care when selecting ammunition for .22 centrefire rifles, many of which are legal for the shooting of muntjac and Chinese water deer in England and Wales, and roe in Scotland. Some of those available over the counter are actually designed for much smaller quarry and are extremely frangible: that is to say that they break up quickly on impact and may not have the penetrative qualities needed for shooting deer. They may also not meet the required muzzle energies or velocities that the law demands for deer.

Opinions vary on the value of bullets with ballistic tips; these incorporate a synthetic tip, which is designed to drive into the core of the bullet on impact and promote expansion. Some stalkers certainly find that, whilst effective, they can cause high levels of meat damage.

If you are still in doubt, just ask any competent riflesmith or an experienced stalker who will be able to guide you in the correct choice.

CHOOSING A STALKING RIFLE

FINDING A RIFLE AND SCOPE COMBINATION
THAT'S RIGHT FOR YOU

Your Firearms Certificate has finally arrived through the post, and you are in a position to actually go out and purchase a rifle. In the excitement of the moment don't, though, walk straight into a gun shop and buy the first one that takes your fancy. You need to think first about what you want of your new rifle and how you intend to use it: make sure you have a really clear idea of what you're looking for before you enter the shop.

First of all, what is your budget? It's easy to spend a great deal of money but if your pockets are not deep plenty of options are still open to you. True, a 'top end' rifle can be expensive, and if you want tack driving accuracy you may need to spend more, but today even mass produced factory rifles should be capable of producing group sizes of below one inch at 100 yards. This is more than adequate for deer stalking.

There are some excellent rifles available at a fraction of the price you might spend on a prestige model, but in truth many of the differences are largely cosmetic. When it comes to the crunch, what really counts is the rifle's ability to shoot accurately and consistently.

As we'll see, the scope is probably the more important part of the set-up so we'll look at that first. Spend as much as you can afford on the highest quality possible. It must be robust enough to absorb the punishing recoil of a full bore rifle and still retain its zero, placing your bullets where you want them time after time. You can get away with a cheaper scope on a .22 rifle or an airgun, but not with a deer rifle.

A 6x42 scope will cover most general stalking needs, and some very experienced stalkers consider 4x magnification to be more than enough. You may be tempted by a variable power scope where the magnification can be increased or reduced according to circumstances. These can offer you great versatility, but beware of cheaper models, which may alter zero at different power settings. It is admittedly very useful to be able to reduce the power in close woodland, where 6x can be too much when the deer is very close and all you can see is brown when trying to sight on a specific point. On more powerful settings, however, remember that as you increase the magnification you will also emphasise any rifle shake, as well as reducing light-gathering abilities. (See *Stalking Optics* on page 96 for more information on this subject.)

Make sure that you are comfortable with the reticule pattern – the 'cross hairs' – as a wide variety is available. A popular choice is a fine centre with thicker posts on the outside, which makes aiming easier in poor light. Don't neglect the scope mounts either. These are the essential connection between scope and rifle, and must be secure and robust enough to do the job properly.

Finally, we can move on to the rifle. I've assumed that you have decided on a straightforward bolt action; there are other options, but this is the popular choice of most deer stalkers for several reasons, not least that it carries its own resupply of spare rounds of ammunition and allows for quick reloading between shots. Will it have a wood or a composite stock, though? Wood is undeniably more attractive, but composites are lower maintenance and less prone to warping. Is your rifle going to be an all-weather workhorse, or used just for occasional recreational stalking? If the former, you may also want to consider a stainless steel barrel rather than a traditional blued one.

Full stock, or stutzen, rifles – with a wooden stock that extends to the end of the barrel – can be very tempting. They are light and manageable but usually come with a very light barrel that will heat up quickly. They are intended for sport hunting when only one or two shots are likely to be taken at any one time. This can be very frustrating on a range when you have to wait for the barrel to cool between strings of shots, and of course you cannot risk the barrel overheating and shifting zero when taking multiple shots during actual culling. Also consider that it is usually impossible to fit a sound moderator to this type of rifle.

A detachable magazine is handy, though not essential. It allows for easy loading and unloading, and a spare one allows you to carry extra ammunition conveniently and ready for a quick reload if necessary. Don't be too concerned if your choice of rifle does not come with traditional iron sights fitted. These are usually rendered redundant by fitting a telescopic sight and, besides, no conscientious deer stalker would wish to use open sights for shooting live quarry when a precision alternative is available.

I hope that you will be fitting a sound moderator, and that you have remembered to ask for one when applying for your FAC as you need separate authority to acquire one. Over the years, moderators have become smaller, lighter and more efficient, and they bring many benefits beyond just protecting your hearing. Hopefully your final choice of rifle has been screw cut to take a moderator in the factory; if not, do be aware that, even if skilfully done by a riflesmith, this could count as a modification to the rifle which might invalidate a manufacturer's guarantee.

By now you'll probably have little change, if any, from at least £1,500 for a new rifle, scope and moderator, and it is easy to spend more than double this figure if your pockets are deep enough. On the other hand, you may wonder if you can actually afford a new set-up. There is always the second-hand option, which is a very good alternative. There are certainly some excellent bargains to be had, but do take care that the barrel has not been shot out, and that the rifle is in proof and fully fit for purpose. Buying from a reputable gun dealer who offers a guarantee and reliable after-sales service is always prudent in such cases.

Before leaving the shop, purchase several brands of appropriate ammunition to try. Don't rely on recommendations from friends who have had good results with their own particular set-up. You'll find that different rifles seem to prefer different loads and perform accordingly. In time you may wish to take up home loading and tailor loads to your specific rifle, but for now it pays to experiment with various manufacturers' offerings and find what works best.

Death is not a terrible thing... not if you respect the thing you kill, not if you kill to feed your people or your memory. **Robert Ruark, *Horn of the Hunter***

COLLIMATORS

A collimator, often known as a scope sighter, or by a number of commercial names such as 'Shot Saver', is an optical device that assists in the zeroing of a rifle. When viewed through the riflescope it shows a grid of vertical and horizontal lines against which the riflescope can be adjusted. Collimators are usually supplied with a variety of mounting rods which can be chosen to suit the calibre of the individual rifle, and which are inserted into the muzzle to hold the collimator in place.

Collimators have two main uses. When a scope is newly mounted to the rifle, it can be adjusted to centre on the collimator grid as an alternative to the slightly cruder method of bore sighting (centring the bore of the rifle onto a fixed point and then adjusting the reticule of the scope to coincide with this). Either method is intended to ensure that the rifle, when fired *without the collimator fitted*, is roughly aligned with the target, allowing finer adjustments to be made by firing further groups of shots.

Once the rifle is shooting to a satisfactory zero, the collimator can be refitted and a note made of where the reticule lies against the grid. From then on it can be used whenever the rifleman wants to check that the reticule has not moved – say, after a long journey or an accidental knock – before he uses the rifle again. To many, this brings considerable peace of mind and saves having to find a range to check-zero the rifle before stalking.

DANGEROUS WILD ANIMALS ACT

In the 1960s and 1970s it became increasingly fashionable to keep exotic species, as well as hybrids such as crosses between dogs and wolves, as domestic pets. This led to considerable concerns over public safety and as a result the Dangerous Wild Animals Act came into being in 1976. Its purpose is to ensure that suitable restrictions exist so that if private individuals choose to keep potentially dangerous animals, they do so in a way that offers no risk to the general public and also takes the welfare of the animals themselves into account. Licences are granted by local authorities, and will specify conditions for the keeping of the animal as well as ensuring that appropriate insurance cover is in place. The list of animals named by the Act is extensive, and includes many species of mammals, birds, reptiles and invertebrates. Zoos, circuses and pet shops are not covered by the Act but must comply with separate regulations.

The only deer specified under the Act are the moose and the caribou or reindeer, although an exception is made for domesticated reindeer. No other deer species are named, so technically you do not need a licence to keep them. Captive deer can of course be very dangerous, especially during the rut, and if they are your property you may have a liability for them, so ensuring that they are kept in appropriate conditions and with suitable insurance cover is important.

A Deranged Deer

A rather flippant stalker I know was called by the management of a local mental hospital. They were a little concerned that a roe deer had entered their extensive gardens.

Quick as a flash he enquired if it thought it was Napoleon. No, came the exasperated reply, it's doing a great deal of damage to the flower-beds, which contain a large number of valuable plants, and what could be done about it?

My friend agreed that he would visit and see what was possible. The deer would be easy to locate, he was told, as it was showing a great deal of interest in the lodge house.

He couldn't resist it. 'Does it want to buy or rent?' he asked.

DEER AS PETS

Under normal circumstances, the close proximity of humans is terrifying to wild deer. Nevertheless, deer occasionally feature as pets, most often as a result of having been found 'abandoned' as fawns and mistakenly taken in by well-meaning people. Usually this is a grave error, which will cost the young deer its life; without specialist knowledge deer can be very difficult to rear successfully and a great many die. It is always best to leave a young animal untouched and where it is, as its mother is usually not far away. If the location is revisited a few hours later she will almost invariably have returned and moved her young elsewhere.

Although a hand-reared female deer can become very tame and docile (some are occasionally encountered in 'petting zoos'), it should never be entirely trusted. Although they do not usually have antlers (see section *Antlered Females* on page 12), female deer are capable of delivering a potentially serious blow with their forefeet if alarmed or put under stress. Male deer, once they have lost their fear of man, can be extremely dangerous and there have been reports of humans who get too close to them being injured or even killed. The hand-reared roe buck has a particular reputation for unexpected ferocity, especially as he matures and starts to become territorial; it is no accident that roe are seldom seen in zoos and collections.

Apart from reindeer, deer have not been domesticated. Generally speaking they do not respond well to being kept in close captivity, although some herding species exist happily in parks where they are given the space they need along with the security of others of their kind. The smaller, more solitary species are more likely to be nervous and skittish. The best place for any deer is in the wild and as such they are not recommended as pets; if they must be kept in captivity, it is best to leave this to the specialists.

Like a dog, he hunts in dreams...   **Alfred, Lord Tennyson,** *Locksley Hall*

DEER IN THE GARDEN

KEEPING DEER AWAY FROM YOUR PRECIOUS PLANTS

With deer numbers on the increase, more and more people are coming into contact with them, even in some surprisingly urban environments. When I lived on the edge of Camberley in Surrey in the early 1990s, we gave up trying to maintain decorative pots at the front of our house after the local roe took to patrolling the street every night and helping themselves to whatever inviting new growth had appeared. These days it is quite possible to see deer, relaxed and unconcerned, couched or feeding in suburban gardens, as they have learned that they are in no significant danger from the human occupants and so have become increasingly bold.

The main species that the gardener is likely to encounter are roe and muntjac, although one cannot rule out visits from others that may be in the vicinity. A friend of mine in the New Forest has virtually given up trying to grow roses and vegetables in the face of nightly onslaughts from a large and hungry fallow population.

Don't be too quick to blame deer for garden damage though – it is quite possible that other animals are responsible, so examine the site for droppings, tracks and other indications of the true culprits. Rabbit droppings are usually round and fibrous; those of deer are cylindrical in shape, smooth and tend to have a small indent in one end while being pointed at the other. Likewise, look at the height and nature of bites through leading shoots. Rabbits, having upper and lower incisor teeth, tend to shear through them cleanly. Deer have no upper incisors, so their bite-marks will have a more ragged appearance.

You have to face it: the only way to really protect your garden from deer is to fence them out, and I'm afraid that a proper deerproof fence is no half-hearted affair. For a start, it has to be high enough. As a general rule of thumb, if a deer can stand on its hind legs and reach the top of a fence with its chin, it can jump it. Even small deer jump well; I know of a muntjac leaping up onto a sheer, five-foot high bank from a standing start.

Your fence also needs to be robust enough to stop a deer tangling its legs, antlers or body in it, with a sufficient gauge of mesh to prevent the animal from squeezing through; for if the head fits, you'd be surprised at how easily the body can follow. Flimsy materials, such as chicken wire or light plastic mesh, should be avoided. Even the smallest breaches, often created by badgers, are quickly exploited and widened.

On one occasion I was called to some local allotments, which, despite a fine high fence, were still being raided by roe. The owners were mystified until I was able to point out numerous creeps the deer were using to get under it. Given the option, a deer will nearly always choose to go under, rather than over, an obstacle. As a result the base must be securely pegged, or better yet buried or folded at a right angle on the outside and turfed over. Again, the smallest gap will give the deer an opportunity to get through. I recall watching a roe doe and her well-grown kids travelling beside a high, chain link fence when they disappeared from view behind some bramble. When they reappeared, they were on the far side of the fence. After the trio had moved off I examined the short section where they had been out of sight. The only place where they could have got through was a small gap a few inches high where the base of the fence did not meet the ground. A few shed hairs confirmed that it had been used.

As a proper deer fence is expensive (you may be looking at about £10 per metre) and unsightly, this option may not be for you; so what are the alternatives? Electric fences can be helpful if circumstances allow them, but do take care if you have pets or children. The wires need to be highly visible and the deer will quickly learn to go over or under them, so a low, stand-off wire will help to deter them. Electric fences, of course, must be regularly checked and maintained if they are to remain effective.

An alternative to fencing is a suitably dense hedging plant. It may not be quite as efficient but can certainly be easier on the eye. The wider it is, the better it will be at deterring deer from jumping it. Some people combine a fence with climbing plants to break up the visual impact; in addition, bear in mind that deer are reluctant to cross obstacles when they cannot see what lies on the other side.

If you have particularly valuable plants and shrubs, you can consider protecting them individually until they are established. Tree tubes, though unattractive, are effective if securely staked and a suitable height, and more decorative guards are available – at a cost. Low, temporary fences can also be used to surround small areas during critical growth periods. Deer do not like jumping into small, enclosed spaces.

There are a number of repellents on the market which can be painted onto a tree or shrub, mainly to prevent bark stripping, but these are only generally used during dormant periods. Once new growth occurs, the new shoots are unprotected and vulnerable.

You could try any number of simple deterrents, although success seems to vary according to the user. A free-roaming dog will keep deer away if this is practical, but do consider neighbours who might not appreciate nightly barking. Lion dung is frequently quoted as effective. If you don't happen to know a friendly zookeeper, pellets containing essence of lion dung are commercially available. I know of one local lady who sends her husband out to relieve himself in the vegetable patch every night before bedtime and she swears that the deer never trouble her plants. Others suggest stringing up small bundles of human hair, contained in old tights, around the garden perimeter (these need replacing regularly as the human scent dissipates after a while). By all means try such methods – they may work for you. The important thing is to keep changing your approach, as deer are remarkably adaptable and quickly learn what is dangerous and what is not.

Finally, some mechanical options you might consider for protecting specific areas: a cheap portable radio, set to a talk (rather than music) station, and wrapped in a plastic bag, will often deter deer. You can also buy a device which connects to a hosepipe and is activated by motion; it sprays a brief but powerful burst of water accompanied by a clattering noise. Deer, like any wild animal, hate anything unexpected. You could also look at motion-activated sonic devices, which can be effective under the right circumstances. There are plenty more such things available; a visit to your garden centre or an internet search will suggest various solutions, any of which are worth trying.

There is no 'one size fits all' solution to the problems caused by deer in gardens. Some people will swear by a method that will be deemed useless by others; so you can only experiment and see what is effective in your own particular circumstances. Good luck, and good gardening!

RECOMMENDED MINIMUM FENCE
AND TREE GUARD DIMENSIONS

Species	Fence Height (note 1)	Fence Mesh Size	Tree Guard Height (note 3)
Muntjac	1.5m	75 x 75mm (note 2)	1.2m
Roe	1.5m	200 x 150mm	1.2m
Fallow & Sika	1.7m	220 x 200mm	1.6m
Red	1.9m		1.8m

Notes:

1. The recommended fence heights should offer at least 95% effective protection against deer.
2. 100 x 100mm mesh is proof against muntjac, but bucks can occasionally get their heads through and snag their antlers.
3. Tree guards should be securely supported by stakes. They can blow over in high winds, and larger deer species will often deliberately push them over.

Trapped Deer

- Occasionally deer will become 'trapped' in fenced areas. Left to their own devices they will usually find their way out the same way that they entered if undisturbed. Leave any gates or other exits open and also available to them.

- Do not be tempted to try and herd a deer out of an enclosed area. It will inevitably panic and run the risk of damaging itself while attempting to escape.

- Smaller deer, such as roe and particularly muntjac, can become trapped by the body in wider mesh fences. Approaching them from the front will often encourage them to back out the way they got in without injuring themselves.

- If a deer is firmly caught in a fence, the combination of its own attempts to free itself and the trauma caused by the close proximity of human rescuers may result in unacceptable stresses and serious injury. In such cases, euthanasia may be a more humane option than release.

DEER MANAGEMENT AND TROPHIES –

CAN THEY EVER GO TOGETHER?

Some time ago I enjoyed being sole stalker on a few hundred acres of prime ground in Hampshire, a perfect mixture of largely arable fields and deciduous woodland with some new plantations, which the owner was keen to see established. I shared the stalking rights with a small shooting syndicate but all of us with sporting interests got along well together. I had a good head of roe on the ground and took a moderate, balanced cull each year. The deer were healthy and body weights were generally high; the trouble was that I never seemed to hold any decent, mature bucks.

The issue lay with the neighbours. On one side of my ground lay a large, commercial estate, which let the stalking for a significant sum of money, and on the other was a farmer who shot indiscriminately. I had no real chance of bringing on any quality bucks, for all they had to do was cross a boundary in any direction and they ended up in a freezer or on somebody's wall. The situation was not helped by the presence of a nature reserve in the immediate vicinity where the deer were never shot. This acted as a sanctuary and breeding reservoir, ensuring that whatever I did actually shoot was immediately replaced by young, unterritorial animals that caused disproportionate damage among the young trees. Try as I might, pure deer management was never really an option; I tried to keep some mature bucks, but my main effort was reduced to just a numbers game, trying to keep the overall roe numbers and sex balance reasonably in proportion to the ground. Encouraging antler quality was out of the question and it was all rather dispiriting.

It was clear from speaking to other local stalkers that I was not alone, then or now. The problem is not so great in areas such as the Highlands of Scotland, where deer are managed on a landscape scale. Further south, though, where land is owned in smaller parcels, neighbouring landowners may have wildly different objectives as far as deer are concerned. My little piece of Hampshire was typical, having to cope with aims varying between 'pure' management, recreational trophy hunting, venison production and, worst of all, no management whatsoever.

Such a situation is not helped by the fact that deer are no respecters of man-made boundaries. People who talk possessively about 'their' deer are only fooling themselves: wild deer belong to nobody in the UK. The deer will range wherever they like and only become actual property once dead. This, then, is where problems can arise.

Human nature does not help. If a stalker is faced with a large, mixed group of deer, offering the chance of a shot, it all too often seems that once the smoke has cleared something big with antlers is left lying on the ground. In the meantime the females in the group are usually allowed to make good their escape and carry on breeding.

Unrestricted trophy hunting is hugely damaging to the dynamics of any deer population, but this is particularly so amongst the larger herding species. Fallow must be one of the most mismanaged species of deer in the UK: I frequently meet stalkers bemoaning the lack of big bucks, even where overall densities are high. In one night session, counting deer with infrared equipment, amongst a total of 290 fallow there was not a single mature male to be seen. Fallow range widely and constantly cross boundaries. Stalkers, not working to a planned cull, are simply taking the best that they can, in the knowledge that if they don't, someone else will.

This situation is not just restricted to fallow. The uncontrolled shooting of big red stags around the edges of the New Forest is another major cause for concern. In 2008 there were at least five master stags rutting in the Forest but in 2013 only one was to be seen. If the deer stayed inside the forest they'd be safe, as the Forestry Commission who manage the cull within the National Park preserve the big stags; but once they step outside it is a different matter. As a result the number of big stags is dwindling and the situation is simply not sustainable.

A further problem is people taking on more stalking than they can handle, or, worse still, only bothering during the buck season and doing nothing, or too little, during the shorter days and less clement weather of the doe season. Few would argue that deer in general are increasing in numbers, with associated problems of environmental damage, deer/vehicle collisions and other conflicts with human activities. This must be addressed, but shooting males alone solves little, as it is the females that really produce the future generations. You can have one buck to any number of mature does and there is a good chance that most, maybe all, will be pregnant by the end of the rut.

So, is there a place for trophy shooting within deer management? Of course there is, just so long as these are taken as part of a balanced cull plan. The acid test is to ask yourself if you are seeing good quality mature animals every year. If the answer is 'yes', you are getting it right, for if your ground is capable of consistently producing good trophies it is a reliable sign that the local management policy is sound. There is a big misconception that you cannot have low deer numbers and trophies; it is maintaining a balance that counts.

Indiscriminate trophy shooting does nothing for the species itself or for balance in general. The need for self-restraint is clear but, just as importantly, so is communicating with your neighbouring landowners to try to agree a common approach. This is where the importance of deer management groups and intelligent discussion, taking everyone's viewpoint into account, comes in. It may not always be possible to achieve complete consensus, but it is usually possible to meet people halfway and at least recognise their objectives as far as the deer are concerned. It is, as the old BT advertisement declared, good to talk.

Greed and indiscriminate shooting ought to have no place in the way that we manage our deer. It is up to all of us as individual stalkers to get things right – for the environment, for our successors and for the ultimate good of the deer themselves. The quote from King George VI that opens every edition of *Shooting Times* could not be more appropriate:

'*The wildlife of today is not ours to dispose of as we please. We have it in trust. We must account for it to those who come after.*'

DEER PREDATORS IN BRITAIN

Since the wolf, brown bear and lynx disappeared from Britain there have been no significant natural predators of healthy adult deer to be found in the wild. Foxes are certainly capable of taking young or weakened roe, though, and there have been occasional documented instances of them acting together to predate on deer having difficulty in snowdrifts; the roe's hooves are poorly adapted to cope with deep snow whereas the fox's broader pads and lighter weight put it at an advantage. Nevertheless such behaviour is very rare and doubtless driven by extreme hunger. Otherwise, although it has been reported that golden eagles are capable of attacking and killing roe, there seems to be no significant natural predation of adult animals.

New-born deer of all species are more vulnerable, however, and foxes and badgers will routinely take them given the opportunity. A female deer can be a formidable opponent to any threat to her fawn, and will often see off potential predators by flailing at them with her sharp forefeet. Wild boar are also known to have a significant impact on mainly young deer on the Continent, although it remains to be seen what effect the more limited populations that exist in Britain have.

Domestic dogs can also be a significant threat to deer if allowed to run uncontrolled, and are responsible for the deaths of many deer annually. The smaller species – namely roe, muntjac and Chinese water deer – are especially vulnerable, although the larger deer are not immune to attack. In Richmond Park alone, around three red or fallow deer are killed by out of control dogs every year.

One should not discount the motor car as a major 'predator' of deer in this country. Although no official figures exist, the National Deer-Vehicle Collisions Project estimates that perhaps as many as 74,000 deer a year are killed by vehicles on our roads; how many are seriously injured to die later of their injuries can only be guessed at.

One does not hunt in order to kill; on the contrary, one kills in order to have hunted... If one were to present the sportsman with the death of the animal as a gift he would refuse it. What he is after is having to win it, to conquer the surly brute through his own effort and skill with all the extras that this carries with it: the immersion in the countryside, the healthfulness of the exercise, the distraction from his job. **Jose Ortega y Gasset,** *Meditations on Hunting*

DELAYED IMPLANTATION

Delayed implantation is the term used to describe the phenomenon whereby the fertilised egg does not immediately implant into the uterus wall immediately after mating. Instead it floats free within the uterus for a long period before implantation takes place, and only then does the foetus start to develop normally. As far as roe deer are concerned, although the rut normally takes place around late July or early August, implantation of the fertilised egg does not occur until December or early January. Kids are then usually born towards the end of May. In this way the period of pregnancy is almost doubled.

Why would the roe deer want to do this? Roe were certainly present in Europe during the Ice Ages, and remains of bones and antlers recovered dating from that time are considered indistinguishable from those of their modern counterparts. It is now believed that delayed implantation evolved around this time when the roe was at an environmental disadvantage compared to larger deer species which produced larger calves. Instead of evolving an increased body size to cope with climatic changes, it seems that the device of delayed implantation was developed instead.

Now, as a result, the roe is the only one of our deer species that habitually ruts during the summer. Once the rut is over, there are still several months of mild weather and good feeding ahead to allow animals to recover their body condition before winter sets in. Equally important, the kids are born at a favourable time of year when food sources are abundant, the climate is likely to be kind, and they have plenty of time to grow to a size and strength that enhances their survival chances for the coming winter.

Delayed implantation (also known as the embryonic diapause) does occur in other mammals too. Kangaroos are known to extend their gestation periods to ensure that they are able to produce sufficient milk for a new youngster if they already have a 'joey' at heel. Seals, some of which only come ashore once a year to give birth, employ it, as do some mustelids (such as stoats and badgers), shrews, skunks, bears and armadillos. The roe is the only deer to do so.

Student Howlers

Marking student assignments, I occasionally come across some interesting ideas. Some are based on simple misunderstandings; for example one informed me that 'Americans are more comfortable with private gun ownership because of the Second Commandment'. In others the computer spellchecker is hopefully to blame. A description of a woodland plant survey, for instance, told of 'wooden enemies' and 'blue bellies'.

Another category of howler suggests a blind over-reliance on the Internet. I was once informed that Chinese water deer cause considerable environmental damage by burrowing into river banks and undermining them. At something of a loss, as this was news to me, I shared the student's contention with a fellow tutor whose specialist area was countryside management. It took us some time to work it out but eventually we realised that the writer had 'cut and pasted' a Wikipedia entry on Chinese mitten crabs.

DEPENDENCY

It is difficult to be truly specific about when a young deer becomes truly independent of its mother. A number of factors have a bearing on this, including local circumstances, the species and the development of the individual itself.

The newborn deer is very dependent on colostrum, which is produced by the mother for some days after giving birth. Colostrum is rich in antibodies, which enhance the immune system and help to protect the calf from disease. Thereafter normal milk is produced. A red deer's milk is considered to contain almost twice the butterfat and three times the protein content of that of a Jersey cow. Unsurprisingly, the calf grows quickly.

Weaning ages vary between species. Muntjac may be weaned at as young as two months old, while red deer can still be taking milk from their mothers more than seven months after birth, and females which have missed a year from breeding may carry on lactating for considerably longer.

The matter does not end with weaning, however. Just as a human child cannot be considered independent simply because it has been weaned at, say, a year old, neither can the young deer. It is just as reliant as the child for guidance and the formative education received from its mother. Although the weaned deer may be capable of surviving on its own, the longer it stays with its dam the better will be its development and its chances of survival. In many species, deer included, the young are eventually driven off physically by the mother as the time to give birth to her next calf approaches.

DIAL 112

Whilst I know that this is not strictly about deer, the emergency number 112 is a potential life-saver to anyone who spends time outdoors, so it is well worth highlighting.

Though the number 999 is specific to emergency calls in the UK, 112 can be used in some 80 countries around the world, including the whole of the European Union. Most of these countries have their own national emergency number as well. In the UK, both the numbers 999 and 112 function in exactly the same way, although 112 does offer some special advantages.

Irrespective of who your mobile phone provider is, dialling 112 will use any tower within your reception area to transmit your message, and will give your call priority if the network is busy. It will also work if you have no credit on a pay-as-you-go phone, or if your contract phone has been blocked for non-payment of bills. With some phones, it will even allow the call if there is no SIM card inserted.

If you have insufficient reception to make a voice call, you can send a text message instead. As texts are very short bursts of transmission, there is a much higher likelihood that you will get through – but you do have to register for this service. Send a text message saying 'Register' to 112: you will receive an automated reply, to which you reply 'Yes'. You will then be able to send text messages from your phone to the emergency services, should this be necessary.

There is a popular misconception that 112 will connect you via satellite. It will not, nor will it enable a satellite to pinpoint your position. For that to happen you would need a special satellite phone, which few people have.

You should not, of course, rely solely on a mobile phone as your only method of emergency communication if you are working alone; phones can malfunction or batteries run down. As a bare minimum, always consider telling someone where you are going, what your route will be and what time to expect you back.

EATING ROADKILL

Every now and then you come across people who advocate collecting and eating animals killed on our roads. Although wild deer are not owned by anybody while still alive, the law is very clear about ownership once they have been killed. The carcase becomes the possession of the person who owns the land, or holds the sporting rights for the land, on which it dies. If it is lying on a public road, therefore, it belongs to the road owner: for practical purposes, this is probably the local council or the Highways Agency. Thus it may not be legally removed by the next passer-by who happens upon it – who could then be liable under civil or possibly criminal law, although this is a very unclear area with each case judged on its merits. There is also the risk of being suspected of poaching if stopped by the police. Incidentally, a motorist who hits a deer is not required to report the incident to the police as they would be if the animal had been, for instance, a domestic dog.

Deer that have not been killed by legal means (effectively by shooting, under the terms of the Deer Act), may not be passed into the human food chain and all wild meat intended for human consumption must be inspected by a trained person against disease or other contamination. People have been known to take road casualties for private consumption but the quality of the venison from an animal hit by a motor vehicle is likely to be very poor. The impact, even if there are few external signs of injury, will probably have caused widespread internal damage, which would contaminate the meat. Furthermore, if the animal is not killed outright by the collision its system will flood with adrenaline as a reaction to stress, tainting the meat and making it bitter and unpalatable.

There is one very significant health and safety issue attached to eating roadkill of which you should be aware. There have been documented cases where a deer has been euthanased by a vet using a lethal injection, then left for collection and disposal, but disappeared in the meantime. In one known instance the person involved fed the liver to his dog, which subsequently died. To date there is no record of a human fatality but the risk is great and must not be discounted.

FALLOW ANTLER PALMATION

Generally speaking, the size of a fallow buck's antlers depend upon his age, but there can be a significant difference in the size and shape of them even within local populations. Although common in the more artificial environments provided by deer parks or other collections, it often seems that 'classic', large, palmated fallow antlers can occur less usually elsewhere.

The social structure of fallow herds may provide a simple explanation for people reporting that big bucks are not being seen: fallow tend to live in single-sex groups for much of the year and the observer may be in an area that is normally populated by doe herds. Although there may be a few male animals amongst them, these are unlikely to be anything other than young ones who have as yet produced only juvenile antlers. Where there are larger, mature bucks in an area, they can be very secretive and virtually nocturnal in their habits: another reason for them not being readily seen. In addition, the over-shooting of mature males – where intelligent deer management, based on the control of female numbers, is not taking place – obviously results in fewer sightings.

Some localities simply do not seem to produce classic, widely palmated fallow antlers regularly. This can be for any number of reasons. The annual growth of these structures demands considerable resources, and if the animal is not finding quality forage, including essential trace elements, it follows that antler growth may not be as impressive as elsewhere. Genetics and stress, be it from such sources as over-population or human pressures, can also affect antler growth.

FALLOW DEER IN BRITAIN

Fallow have been present in Britain for so long that they are considered native, but those we have here now actually originated in the Mediterranean region. Recent archaeological discoveries at Fishbourne Roman Palace in West Sussex point to the Romans importing the species during the first century AD and maintaining a captive population, both as a status symbol and as a food source. Radiocarbon dating of fallow bones found at Fishbourne has placed them as early as AD 60.

Whether any of these escaped captivity and established a feral population is, however, uncertain, and their presence in this country between then and the Norman Conquest remains a matter for conjecture.

There is no doubt that the Normans were responsible for widespread introductions in the eleventh century and it is generally accepted that these are the origin of the fallow's great success as a feral species. Their popularity as a park deer has also aided this spread. Fallow are a very attractive species and a natural choice for those who wished to enhance their deer parks with an animal that was not only decorative but also had an important food value. Their widespread popularity provided multiple points of introduction through both deliberate releases and escapes and the fallow has flourished as a result. Many localised feral herds are still associated with areas that held, or still have, adjacent deer parks.

To say that fallow did not exist at all in Britain before the Romans is not entirely true. Fossil evidence has proved that the species was widespread throughout Europe around a hundred thousand years ago but became extinct during the last glaciation, with only a few pockets of populations surviving in some less affected southern areas. From these remnants the fallow has spread, largely with human help, to once again become a successful species not just in Britain but across much of Europe too. Even further afield, they have been introduced to parts of North and South America, Australia, New Zealand, and the West Indies.

Killer Roebuck

It was a very hot summer this particular year, and the roe rut was all but over. A group of us had gathered for a pint before heading home after stalking one evening when one of our number, recently returned from Africa, started to recount his hunting adventures. After a while these started to get rather tiresome but the speaker didn't seem to realise that his audience was becoming impatient. He moved on to the tale of following up a wounded waterbuck, stressing just how much of a reputation for aggression this particular antelope species has. A member of the group spoke up at this point to say that in fact he had almost been killed by an especially big roebuck the previous day.

'Really, did it go for you?' asked the African hunter incredulously. 'No' came the reply. 'I had to carry it for three miles off Salisbury Plain.'

FINDING STALKING

Perhaps you're looking for your own piece of ground. Maybe you want to stalk on a more regular basis, or even move on to actually managing a deer population. As things stand, you have two main options: try to find somewhere at low cost, or be prepared to pay the going rate for a sporting lease.

The lease is probably the easiest to find but definitely liable to cost more. You may be lucky, but you must be prepared to be bound by a contract and to pay for the privilege. Dependent on location and the quality of the stalking offered, costs can vary considerably. Scan the advertisements in the sporting press or contact a local sporting agent or the Forestry Commission, and you'll probably turn up something quickly enough. Why not consider forming a syndicate to spread the cost? Too many stalkers take on land that they can't reasonably manage on their own. If you can't take on the available ground full-time, why not consider the BASC stalking schemes?

If you are lucky, you can find something more reasonable. Be prepared to put in some leg-work, and use your local knowledge. Spread the word that you are looking for ground: gamekeepers, fellow beaters and game dealers are all good starting points. By all means visit local landowners, but choose your time carefully – they are busy people. Think of your appearance too. A smartly-dressed, polite approach is more likely to bear fruit than rolling up in the farmyard dressed in camo, ready to go with a rifle over your shoulder and an out-of-control spaniel.

The landowner probably doesn't know you from Adam so first impressions really count. Competence and safety are everything, along with the reassurance of responsible deer management. Sound qualifications help too – DSC1 or 2, or BDS Deer Manager are a good start – as well as insurance. He has got to want you on his ground, so offer a reasonable return for his hospitality. These days, a bottle of whisky at Christmas simply isn't enough unless you are very, very fortunate.

Sometimes, opportunities do come out of the blue. A local farmer called a while back to ask if I could reduce the deer on his land as it wasn't stalked and he had noticed the numbers building up. There was no question of money changing hands in this case – all he wanted was someone he could trust and to share the shot deer on a 'one for you, one for me' basis. How had he got my name? From none other than the local game dealer, who recommended me simply because of the quality of the carcases I took in to him.

So don't give up hope. Play your cards right and sometimes the stalking will actually come to you.

Deer hunting would be fine sport, if only the deer had guns.   **W S Gilbert**

FOLLOWING UP

WHAT TO DO WHEN A SHOT DOESN'T GO AS PLANNED

The moment has come. You've finally got into a position where you judge that a shot at the deer in front of you is possible; the range is good, you're in a comfortable shooting position, and you know that a good backstop of soft earth awaits behind your target to receive the bullet. The cross hairs of the scope drift into position; you steady yourself, exhale slightly and squeeze the trigger.

Hopefully the deer will drop instantly, or make a short blundering run before falling dead in plain view. Sometimes, though, things don't go quite as we intend and it will be necessary to follow up the animal. Rather than rushing in and potentially making matters worse, now is the time to make an intelligent appraisal of the situation and act accordingly.

If a deer reacts to a shot by running off, this is not necessarily a cause for worry. It's a perfectly normal reaction. By placing your bullet into one of the vital organs, the deer's brain is starved of oxygen as its blood supply is shut off. Unconsciousness and death will follow very rapidly, but in the meantime the animal's natural instinct to flee may take over, especially if the animal was on the alert when hit. Be in no doubt that the chest shot is the most humane option as the heart, lungs and major blood vessels surrounding them offer the largest target with a significant margin for error; by contrast, head and neck shots can be fraught with danger. These are very small and mobile targets, and should only be considered by experienced stalkers who are totally confident in their equipment and abilities. Such shots are certainly not recommended for the average stalker, as the slightest error could result in a badly wounded deer that will be difficult to find and finish off easily.

Once you have taken the shot, reload immediately in case another is needed. Now is the time to watch and think. Don't move just yet; the fact that you have just fired a shot means that there is already a safe backstop if you need to shoot again. Your next steps will now depend on the situation facing you, which will probably fall into one of the following three scenarios.

With luck, as I said, the deer is down in plain sight. This should not pose a problem, but never assume that an animal is dead until you have proved it. Watch it for a couple of minutes, and if it shows no signs of moving approach it carefully, keeping a suitable backstop available and be ready to shoot again quickly if it shows signs of life. Touch it on the eyeball with your stalking stick – if there is no blink reaction, the animal is dead. Now is the time to unload your rifle and prepare to perform the gralloch.

An alternative outcome may be that you have seen the deer fall, but cannot see where it is lying because of, say, long grass. Once again, there is no rush. Stay where you are for a good few minutes before approaching as before, but this time take special care to stay downwind and be especially cautious. Even a mortally wounded deer can be galvanised into getting up and running by the sudden unexpected appearance of a human.

The third, and most potentially difficult, situation is that the shot animal has made off into cover. Hopefully you will have observed its reaction to being hit and have an idea of what has happened. A solid thump of the bullet hitting, followed by the animal bucking or kicking out with its hind legs before rushing off with head held low, are classic indicators of a good hit in the heart or lungs. If this is so you can reasonably expect the animal to be lying dead close by. A hollow thud, on the other hand, suggests a hit further back on the body. In such cases the deer may hunch its back and move off rather more slowly. If it is safe, shoot again immediately – this is one of the few occasions when it is acceptable to shoot at a moving animal. Before moving forward, however, allow a waiting time appropriate to the circumstances. If the deer has been hit in the liver, you will probably find it dead if you allow fifteen minutes or so. An animal wounded in the gut may take longer to expire but will probably lie down fairly soon and should be allowed about thirty minutes to stiffen up before you attempt to approach it – this will mean less chance of it getting up and running on, and give you a better opportunity for a finishing shot if needed.

Signs of a hit that will not be immediately fatal, such as a hanging jaw or swinging leg, demand a quick second shot if possible. These animals need to be followed up immediately, preferably with a good dog, as they are likely to travel a long distance at speed before settling. In such cases be careful of crossing estate boundaries – you may find yourself guilty of armed trespass if you don't have the agreement of your neighbours to do so.

Before moving forward, take care to mark your firing position so that you can find it again if you need to retrace your steps. Always make sure that you are in a position to fire again if you need to in a hurry, and slowly approach the place where the deer was standing when it was hit. Don't expect to find blood and hair exactly on the spot; it's often surprising how far the exiting bullet can throw them. Blood sign will give you a fair indication of what to expect. Plenty of bright red arterial blood, or frothy pinker blood containing pieces of pink lung tissue, are excellent signs of a mortal hit and the deer should be lying dead nearby. Very little blood, green stomach contents or long shards of leg bone are a warning that you are going to have to be more careful in your follow up.

Once again, this would be a good time to employ the services of a proven tracking dog. If you don't have one, you will obviously need to cope on your own. Mark the place where the blood trail begins, then search meticulously for further drops of blood; it can be surprising how difficult they can be to see at times. Mark them with a small piece of tissue paper to make them more visible, and don't just look at the ground – examine any foliage that the deer may have brushed against leaving blood from the exit wound, and remember that wounded deer tend not to run in a straight line. Try not to spoil the blood trail by trampling over it as it may be necessary to bring in a dog later if you are unsuccessful. At all times, use your binoculars to check what lies ahead, and don't be tempted to search around blindly in the hope that you will stumble over your deer.

All being well, you will find your animal. If it is not dead, far better to stand off and shoot it again rather than move in closer with a knife: it might have enough strength to spring up and run off, or flail around with antlers or hooves (sika have a particular reputation for being aggressive when wounded). Never, ever, assume a complete miss until you have searched diligently. Once again, a good dog is invaluable and all conscientious stalkers should either own one or at least have one available on call.

Following up is not difficult. It's simply a matter of observation and interpretation of the signs available to you; read them sensibly, go carefully and if you follow these guidelines you should find your deer.

Location of Bullet Strike	Common Deer Reaction	Usual Blood Sign	Recommended Stalker Action
HEART	Variable. May fall immediately, or rear up, lash out with hind legs, stand and 'shiver' etc before walking a short distance and collapsing, or running off at speed with head held low before collapsing after 30–150m	Bright red and thick	If deer is visible and not moving, approach cautiously ready to fire again if necessary
LUNG		Light red and frothy, possibly containing lung tissue	If deer cannot be seen, wait 10 minutes before commencing follow-up

Location of Bullet Strike	Common Deer Reaction	Usual Blood Sign	Recommended Stalker Action
LIVER	Makes off stiffly	Dark brown	Treat as gut shot if no blood sign seen, otherwise leave for at least 15 minutes before following up
GUT	Deer hunches its back and makes off towards cover	Thin red blood mixed with green stomach contents	Shoot again immediately if possible; otherwise leave for 30 minutes before following up
SPINE	Drops instantly; may roll on back or thrash about	Very little blood	Shoot again immediately if animal shows any sign of getting up
LEG	May drop before recovering and moving off at speed on three legs	Very little blood; long splinters of bone	Shoot again immediately if possible, and follow up (preferably with a dog) without delay
JAW	May fall or show little reaction before moving off at speed, possibly with jaw hanging slack	Very little blood; teeth or bone fragments	

Meat isn't murder, it's delicious. **John Lydon** (aka Johnny Rotten of 1970s punk group the Sex Pistols)

FOSSIL DEER

Deer are thought to be descended from the *Palaeomerycidae*, an extinct family of ruminants which were widespread during the Eocene and Miocene epochs and probably existed for about fifty million years before finally dying out some five million years ago. Their fossils have been found in countries as far apart as Spain, Kazakhstan and Nebraska, USA. They are also considered to be the forbears of modern animals such as the giraffe.

The first deer started to appear alongside the *Palaeomerycidae*. One of the first truly deer-like ruminants was *Eumeryx*, which lived around thirty-five million years ago. In common with modern musk deer and Chinese water deer, it had no antlers but had developed canine tusks. Antlered deer as we know them today did not appear until about twenty million years ago, during the early Miocene. *Dicroceros* was one of these, an important development in deer evolution because it is the first evidence of a deer that shed and regrew its antlers annually rather than bearing permanent horns. Its antlers were simple structures, little more than small forks, and it had small tusks, much like those our modern muntjacs and tufted deer have.

Deer gradually increased in size and developed increasingly complex antlers. The giant deer, genus *Megaloceros*, probably represents the peak of this development. The largest of these deer, *M. giganteus*, stood over six feet high at the shoulder and had massive palmated antlers spanning about fourteen feet. Often referred to as the Giant or Irish Elk (the latter because a significant number of the fossils found have been in Ireland, thanks primarily to the unusually good geological conditions that exist to preserve them there), it lived on the open plains of Europe and Asia during the Ice Age. There are many theories as to why the species finally died out: climate change, over-specialisation or disease have all been suggested.

The deer that we see today reflect the massive changes that have occurred since *Eumeryx* made its first appearance, and distinct families have developed and evolved. The fallow, for instance, with its sophisticated antlers and complex herd structure, has only existed in the form that we know it for the last hundred thousand years. The roe goes back around one million years, and the muntjac, surely one of the most primitive living deer, has seen little change in its appearance for well over fifteen million years.

HIGH SEATS AND PLANNING PERMISSION

A high seat is only a temporary structure and you should not need planning permission to erect one, especially if it is for the protection of forestry or agricultural crops, although of course you should always consult the landowner first. You also need to be aware of a few obligations. If anyone, whether they are authorised or not, injures themselves when using one of your seats you may find yourself held liable, so it is necessary to pay due regard to its construction, siting and maintenance and to comply fully with health and safety regulations and other relevant legislation.

You will be able to reduce the risks of liability by taking a few sensible precautions. First of all, ensure that the seat is properly designed and constructed. Treated timber is best if you are building your own. It goes without saying that all materials which have to bear weight must be of a suitable strength; pay special attention to uprights, rungs, spars and flooring materials. Build in safety features, such as wire-mesh stapled across wooden floors or on ladder rungs to reduce the chances of slipping, and make sure that the rungs themselves are wired or otherwise reinforced against breakage. The seat itself should be stable and secure; if the structure is of a lean-to design, use rope or a ratchet strap, not nails or screws, to secure it to the tree.

Keep a written record of the exact location of all your seats, and ensure that you conduct regular inspections to confirm that they are serviceable. Any seat that is not fit for use should be repaired or removed without delay. A record of these inspections and the maintenance undertaken should also be kept.

A removable ladder is a good way to prevent unauthorised use; another is to cover the rungs with a padlocked plank so that no part of the ladder can be accessed when the seat is not in use. Of course it makes good sense to site a seat well out of public view, and well away from footpaths or any other areas of public access. Finally, it is very important to ensure that every seat is clearly labelled with a suitable sign indicating that it is not for public use.

HOW FAST CAN DEER RUN?

Deer do not normally waste energy by running, preferring to trot if in a hurry but under no threat. When alarmed, however, they are capable of travelling at very considerable speeds, albeit usually in relatively short bursts. Under strict test conditions, white-tailed deer have registered top speeds of around 32 miles per hour, although it has been claimed that they can reach more than 36 mph. For its size, the moose is surprisingly fast; one has been timed travelling 400 metres at 37 mph.

The wapiti or North American elk has been recorded as travelling at 43 mph. Although there are no official figures for the smaller but closely related red deer, in 1970 a frightened stag was captured on a police speed camera running at 42 mph after straying onto the streets of Stalybridge in Cheshire. History does not record whether or not it received a speeding ticket.

Roe deer are probably the most likely deer to be able to sustain high speeds for the longest time and often reach up to 40 mph. There is a claim in *The Guinness Book of Records* that they can maintain speeds of between 30 and 40 mph for distances of up to 20 miles, but how these figures were obtained is not known and it does seem that the very long distance quoted might be open to question.

Many predatory animals can certainly move faster than deer over shorter distances, but tend to be capable of doing so only in very limited bursts of speed before tiring quickly. A deer finds its best defence in alertness, agility and being able to maintain its top speed over much longer distances.

HOW MANY YOUNG DO DEER HAVE?

Generally speaking, the larger the deer (in the UK at least) the fewer young they tend to have. Certainly, red, sika and fallow normally give birth to only a single calf (or fawn, as the young fallow is known) each year, whereas roe and Chinese water deer more usually produce multiple young (known as kids and fawns respectively). The muntjac is the exception to the 'size' rule of thumb – although the smallest UK deer species, they produce only a single fawn at each birthing.

Twins, although unusual among the larger deer species, are by no means unknown and do appear from time to time. The casual onlooker may occasionally be deceived by the sight of a fallow doe allowing a fawn which is not her own to suckle, giving the impression that she is nursing twins.

Roe deer usually do give birth to twins, although triplets are not uncommon if the doe is in particularly good condition. Whether all three young, who may be slightly smaller than is normal at birth, survive their first few weeks of life depends largely on the weather conditions, but in good years there is no reason why they should not do so.

Chinese water deer, one of our smallest British deer, have the potential to be the most prolific breeders. Up to seven young have been recorded from a single birthing, though this is admittedly unusually high: two or three is more normal. There are currently no confirmed records of surviving muntjac twins in this country; however, there have been rare instances of muntjac does carrying twin foetuses and uncorroborated (so far) suggestions of live twins. As the muntjac is such a secretive deer that hesitates to leave thick cover, twins are certainly possible and should not be dismissed out of hand despite the previous statement!

HUMAN ACTIVITY AND DEER

Like any other prey species, deer have to be able to differentiate between what is, and what is not, a potential threat. If they cannot do this, then they will spend their lives fleeing unnecessarily, wasting valuable energy and time that would otherwise be spent feeding or resting.

That deer learn quickly about the potential threat that human activities pose is very evident. A human figure on the Scottish hill can quickly cause red deer to clear the area, whereas the red deer of the New Forest have learned not to be excessively alarmed by the large number of visitors to this popular National Park. Roe and muntjac, normally shy and retiring, are increasingly becoming associated with the gardens of suburbia, frequently in broad daylight and in full view of the occupants of houses. Elsewhere, mechanical deterrents, such as 'gas guns', flashing lights or scarecrows, can quickly become ineffective as the deer learn that they pose no real threat.

If deer are put under continual pressure by hunting and other forms of disturbance they find threatening, then they will naturally become more wary and skittish, often changing their habits completely. Interestingly, the roe deer on the Army firing ranges of Salisbury Plain have become habituated to the explosions of artillery shells. Instead of fleeing wildly when the big guns start firing, they have learned to spend the day laid up close by and then move back out into the impact area to feed soon after the day's firing has ceased.

Zoo Time

During my later years at school I was fortunate to work at weekends and during holidays at a small, family-owned zoo not far from my home in North Wales. I seem to remember that the pay was a pound a day, which didn't go very far even in the mid 1970s, but it was fun, varied and interesting.

You were, of course, constantly in the public eye but this occasionally got forgotten. One of the less pleasant Saturday morning jobs was the cleaning of the bear pit, a task invariably reserved for fellow student worker Mike and myself.

On one occasion, with a transistor radio propped on a log to entertain us while we shovelled and wheelbarrowed, we launched into an impromptu performance of The Funky Gibbon, only to look up at the polite applause and see a row of heads peering at us from the viewing platform. The zoo had opened its gates a little early that day.

I also recall a wrestling match with a spider monkey over the possession of a pot of paint with which I was touching up its enclosure – they may be small, but they are certainly quick, strong and tenacious. Another time I had to rugby-tackle a king vulture which had slipped its jesses on the bird of prey weathering ground. Both these incidents took place in front of amused and appreciative audiences: another, however, did not go down quite so well.

The deer paddock lay at the bottom of a slippery and steeply sloping hill, and getting a motor vehicle down to it was out of the question. So Mike and I felt some dismay when we were despatched to remove the carcase of an old fallow doe that had been ailing for a while and had eventually died during the night. We stood looking at the carcase, wondering how best to transport it to the top, when Mike had a flash of inspiration and went to get an eight-foot larch pole.

Half an hour later we were on the carpet in the curator's office. The paying public, it seemed, had taken great exception to the sight of the two of us packing the animal out with its feet tied together and suspended under the pole on our shoulders, singing an out of breath version of 'Robin Hood, Robin Hood, riding through the glen...' as we carried it up the hill to the waiting pickup.

HUMMELS

Red deer stags that do not grow antlers are normally referred to as 'hummels' (the word is derived from humble). The condition is relatively uncommon; in one study in Scotland it was found that perhaps one stag in three hundred was a hummel. It has often been suggested that a hummel, not having to expend body resources on growing new antlers every year, will always be bigger than a 'normal' stag but in fact this is not necessarily the case. Although some hummels with very heavy body weights do occur, they can be found in a variety of sizes.

Studies suggest that hummelism is almost certainly linked to poor initial development in the red deer calf. It is certainly most strongly associated with red deer in the Highlands of Scotland where these animals tend to live in habitats with very poor available nutrition compared to conditions further south. Normally, a male calf will start to grow his first set of antlers at around eight months old. This is reliant on the calf having already developed pedicles, the bony projections on the skull from which the antlers grow. Production of pedicles is linked to the calf reaching a threshold body weight of around fifty-six kilograms. If this weight is not reached by the time the calf is about six months old, subsequent antler development is affected even if the deer grows normally thereafter.

Although any young deer which suffers testicular damage before reaching puberty will find its ability to develop pedicles, and subsequently antlers, impaired, this is not necessarily the case with hummels which are usually fertile. Hummels frequently hold hinds during the rut and breed successfully, although they will be at a serious disadvantage if challenged by an antlered rival. Their offspring are usually normal antlered animals. Hummelism is not considered to be linked to genetic factors.

Experiments on grown hummel stags, which have involved deliberately damaging the pedicle area to simulate seasonal antler casting, have actually stimulated subsequent antler growth. In some cases this has resulted in sustained regular casting and regrowth, following the normal annual cycle.

Whilst hummelism is most commonly associated with red deer, it has been seen in other species, specifically white-tailed and mule deer, and woodland caribou. In the south-west of England, a hummel is often referred to as a nott stag whilst in Germany the term *plattkopf*, literally 'flat head', is used.

Elk were mating now – the males were fighting, and they had to chase the females, which depleted the fat that both sexes had accumulated over the summer and thereby diminished their chances of surviving the winter. 'It would be better for the elk,' Dave said, as we prepared dinner, 'if the females just gave it up.' All three women stared at him. A silence ensued. Dave said, 'Or I could be wrong.' **Tim Cahill, *Lost in My Own Backyard: A Walk in Yellowstone National Park***

HYBRIDISATION

Hybridisation between two different species is very rare under natural conditions, and even the progeny are unlikely to be fertile unless the parents are genetically close. Generally speaking, different species are only really likely to interbreed when they do not have access to others of their own, and as a result most hybridisation tends to happen under enclosed conditions such as in zoos and parks.

The only deer species known to hybridise readily in Britain are the red and the sika, which are very closely related, both being members of the *Cervus* genus of deer. There is a substantial size difference however, and successful matings are only likely to take place between sika stags and red hinds. It is generally considered that such hybridisation is brought about by population imbalances: for example, where there are no red stags holding hind parcels, a wandering sika stag may take advantage of the situation. Interestingly, in deer parks where balanced populations of red and sika deer live in close proximity, hybridisation does not appear to be an issue. Among our native red deer, however, it is becoming of increasing concern as their genetic integrity is considered to be under significant threat.

Our other deer species are so genetically distant from each other that hybridisation is extremely unlikely. Nevertheless, there have been some rather fanciful claims over the years. Red deer have been variously suggested as having successfully mated with horses, cows and fallow deer, while as recently as 1974 a cross between a roe buck and a domestic sheep was reported in Northumberland. None of these claims have been proven and it is highly unlikely that they were genuine.

LIFE SPANS

The natural life spans of different deer species vary widely, and much depends on various factors. These might include prevailing weather conditions or the quantity and quality of available food, but ultimately tooth wear is the cause of death. Deer teeth do not regenerate – once they have been worn down to a point where foodstuffs cannot be fully broken down to allow the digestive system to extract nutrition efficiently, the animal's condition declines rapidly.

Among British deer, as a general rule of thumb the larger species live longer. Wild red deer in some parts of the country have been recorded as reaching some twenty years of age, although under more harsh Highland conditions it is estimated that only a quarter of animals live past the age of eight. Fallow and sika, especially under milder southern conditions, seem to average a lifespan of around fifteen years.

In studies carried out in southern England, the majority of roe deer were shown to average about eight years of age, although some animals lived to as old as twelve. Under most circumstances, ten is probably a very respectable age for a roe to achieve. The same sort of life span seems to apply to muntjac. In Britain, wild muntjac, tagged as mature animals, have been recovered dead some ten years later. The shortest-lived of our deer is the

Chinese water deer, which, being smaller and less well-adapted to British conditions, seldom lives beyond the age of six years in the wild.

Deer fare rather better in captivity, where living tends to be easier and a better quality of nutrition is available to them. One captive muntjac doe lived for nineteen years, and the larger deer species have all been recorded as exceeding an average twenty years of age. A notable red deer was a Richmond Park hind, tagged as a calf in 1969, who died just before Christmas 1996, aged twenty-seven years and six months.

LIVING WITH INJURIES

Deer are incredibly robust animals and can sustain injuries that would be totally debilitating to many humans, yet still manage to recover and carry on with their lives. One can only marvel at and admire their ability to do so. Three-legged deer are noted all too often, and observers never fail to marvel at their ability to keep up within a herd, travel swiftly across rough ground, or even compete with more able-bodied deer for preferred feeding. Males have been known to rut successfully, while females have given birth to and successfully raised their young to maturity.

The causes of lost limbs can be many and varied, and we can only guess at them in many cases – collisions with motor vehicles or entanglement in wire are two common ones. If the deer survives the initial trauma, it will often adapt quickly to life on three legs. In Britain there are no natural predators to take advantage of the animal's weakened state, giving it the opportunity to recover and lead a relatively normal life. Elsewhere, of course, it is more likely to fall prey to predators, which will very quickly single it out as being at a disadvantage.

A good example of just how well a deer can cope with only three legs is that of a large summer roe buck culled in Wiltshire because its right foreleg was missing. When examined, the stump proved to be completely healed over and it was clear that this was an old injury, probably incurred during the previous winter. Otherwise the buck was in prime condition and full of fat, and its weight rivalled the largest roe bucks recorded for the locality in question. In fact, since losing the foreleg, it had even managed to grow an impressive set of antlers which later measured as a gold medal trophy – although, as is often typical in such cases, the opposite antler to the injury (thus on the left side) showed considerable deformation.

MANAGING THE CULL

Maybe you've taken the plunge and are no longer a recreational stalker shooting within the confines of an agreed cull plan – you're creating the plan yourself. Despite the new responsibilities that come with the title of deer manager, don't worry: it is not a science but rather an art, for which you will develop a 'feel' as you gain experience. If you are lucky, you'll have someone experienced to guide you. If not, there is plenty of reading material available, or you might book a place on the excellent BDS Deer Management course. There is plenty of help out there if you're new to the challenge.

Managing a deer population follows a time-honoured process – namely count, plan, and cull. You can't conduct an informed cull without knowing what sort of deer numbers (and species) you have on the ground and then weighing that information against the sort of population the ground can reasonably support. And don't just think in terms of lush summer growth with abundant forage for the deer: you must plan for the worst-case conditions of winter too.

You also need a very clear idea of your objectives before you start planning. Do you want increased carcase weights, a reduction in crop damage, better trophies? The list can go on. Very often your stalking landlord will dictate these aims anyway. Once you have all the necessary information to hand, there is any number of ways to access professional guidance, including IT programs for the computer-literate.

Consider, too, how much time you are going to be able to devote to your deer. You will quickly find that the key to getting numbers to the right level – and keeping them there – lies in culling females. For these, the open season is short, the days shorter, and the weather is frequently dreadful. You may well need some assistance. Choose your stalking friends carefully and they will be a real asset. Don't forget to liaise with your neighbours as well – deer are no respecters of man-made boundaries.

Don't neglect record keeping, by the way. Records need not be complicated, perhaps showing little more than larder weights, parasitic burdens and antler development, plus anything else in particular that you might want to include. Consider also producing a written report of the year's activities. Both accounts will show your landlord that you are doing a serious job of work and also provide you with valuable historical comparisons. In the longer term, they will show just how successful your management policies have been – very useful when the lease comes up for renewal, or if the landowner receives a more tempting cash offer for the stalking rights.

Above all, don't be put off by the responsibilities of cull management. Moving up a gear from recreational stalker to manager may seem to be a major one, but it's a natural and hugely satisfying step for the committed deer enthusiast.

The Four Rules of Gun Safety

Rule One – All guns are always loaded.

Rule Two – Never let the muzzle cover anything you are not willing to destroy.

Rule Three – Keep your finger off the trigger until your sights are on target.

Rule Four – Be sure of your target. Know what it is, what is in line with it, and what is behind it. Never shoot anything you have not positively identified.

Jeff Cooper, *Art of the Rifle*

MATERNAL INSTINCTS

In the woods where my wife rides her horse, the deer are usually quick to move away when riders appear. One morning, though, a roe doe stood her ground, stamping her feet occasionally, when the horses appeared and only moved off when they got to within a few feet of her.

This happened in mid-May and there was little doubt that the doe had recently given birth, and that her kid was hidden close by. At such times maternal instincts can be very strong and will often override a deer's natural inclination to flee from danger.

It is not unknown for dogs and other carnivores to be chased by a protective doe, who will use her sharp forefeet to flail at the offender and inflict serious injury if she gets close enough. Roe does have been seen to drive off foxes that they considered to be a threat to their offspring, and one observer witnessed a dog fox actually killed by a blow from a doe's forefoot during such an encounter. This behaviour is not just restricted to the roe; any female deer with vulnerable young can be capable of considerable bravery when defending them. People involved in tagging park calves, especially, have learned to keep a sharp lookout for aggressive mother deer.

Once she has fawned, the doe will have eaten the afterbirth – probably to reduce the chances of a predator discovering the site – and licked the new-born's coat clean. This serves both to dry the coat and to stimulate circulation. At this point the parental bond is established; it is strong to the point that the mother is extremely unwilling to abandon her offspring. After birth, a young deer will be left concealed while its mother feeds until strong enough to accompany her. If disturbed it can scream loudly and that usually causes her to return to it quickly if she is within earshot. Any perceived threat will provoke an aggressive display, which can include barking and foot-stamping.

If some animals are good at hunting and others are suitable for hunting, then the Gods must clearly smile on hunting. **Aristotle**

MINERAL LICKS

The practice of providing mineral licks for wild deer has long been an established practice on the Continent, although it has not proven so popular in the UK. That deer need trace elements to develop their physical condition and antlers is beyond question. However, they usually obtain these elements through regular natural foraging and should not need artificial supplements under normal circumstances.

Mineral licks are regularly credited with assisting in improved body weights of adult animals and subsequently birth rates. There have certainly been recorded instances of male deer that regularly visit them producing antlers of a higher than normal standard for the local population. The best way to establish a lick is to fix the mineral block to the top of a post or tree stump; as the block is dissolved by the rain it will run down the post onto the ground where it is more readily taken. The addition of an attractant, such as aniseed, may help to draw the deer to them.

Some deer species seem to take more easily to licks than others. In Britain, fallow tend to visit them most readily, whereas roe seem much less likely to touch them. Even wild deer in Scotland appear reluctant to use them even in poorer habitats. Deer of all species on the Continent are rather more accustomed to using them but this could simply be down to conditioning to the habit by a longer history of their provision by deer managers and estates.

By all means try a mineral lick or two on your ground; if your deer get used to them they will provide useful opportunities for observation, but be aware that the deer will learn quickly to avoid them if culling takes place at the site. If vital trace elements are deficient in the area, for whatever reason, licks may well prove beneficial but results may be mixed. Ultimately, if a managed deer population is kept in balance with the environment that supports it, there should be no vital need to supplement the natural forage available.

A Late-for-work Excuse

It was summer 2002, and I was working at the time for a charming colonel in the Royal Military Police who was about to retire. Throughout his career he had heard countless excuses, but even he had to admit that on this occasion I came up with the best one that he had heard in almost forty years in uniform.

It was quite possible to get in an early morning stalk and still be home and change in time to start work at Headquarters on time, but occasionally something would crop up and I would call in to say that I would be a little late; Colonel Tony was very forgiving about this, and as a result a boss to be treasured. On this particular day I had been unsuccessful with the deer but bumped into a group of people as I drove off the patch. One of them recognised me: Harry was now running a security firm after his spell in the Army, but today was conducting survival training for the girl with him, a family friend who was about to do what he described as a 'survival challenge' in Australia. He made the introductions but thanks to the Army my hearing has never been good and I missed her name. Her face was very familiar, though.

Would I show the girl how to paunch and skin a rabbit, I was asked? I was happy to help out. The girl, pretty, about thirty years old and with what you might describe as a 'Sloane Ranger' accent, was soon getting stuck in despite her obvious distaste for the task. I continued to wonder exactly who she was but felt too embarrassed to ask. Still, I admired her for forcing herself to do something that she clearly hated. Rabbits are pretty pungent at the best of times.

With the bunnies completed, we moved on to gutting trout and red snapper, a fish you don't usually come across in the depths of Hampshire. 'We picked them up at Fortnum's' Harry explained. At this point the alarm bells in my head were starting to ring loudly. Who on earth was she, I wondered? Soon the session drew to an end and we chatted for a while. Harry noticed that I had a camera in the car and wondered if I could take a few photographs 'for publicity'. The alarm bells were clamouring now, but still I couldn't place the girl.

In that pre-digital age I had a roll of twenty-four exposures in the camera and it was not until I had taken the twenty-third that, finally, I realised who it was I had been dressing game with in the woods so far from her usual Kensington haunts. Nobody was going to believe me, so I had to ask Harry to take the last exposure of the two of us together.

I rang work to say that, once again, I'd be a little late in, and Colonel Tony answered. 'Very well,' he said good-humouredly. 'What is it this time?' I had known him for a long while but this was the first and only occasion when I found him lost for words.

'I'm skinning rabbits,' I took enormous pleasure in announcing, 'with Tara Palmer-Tomkinson.'

(The 'survival challenge', by the way, turned out to be the first series of the popular television show I'm a Celebrity ... Get Me Out of Here! In it Tara, 'It Girl', socialite, television presenter, model, newspaper columnist and darling of the tabloid press was eventually runner-up to disc jockey Tony Blackburn after enduring a series of trials including 'bug showers'. She didn't have to skin any more rabbits though.)

MODERATION IN ALL THINGS

A thought struck me on the ranges recently. Out of some twenty rifles in use on the firing point, only one was unmoderated – and the crash of noise it made was the source of a great deal of good-natured ribbing from the other firers, whose rifles were almost silent in comparison. How different to the situation only a few years ago, when the moderated rifle would have been the exception rather than the norm.

The suppressor, or sound moderator, has only come into popular sporting use in recent years even though the first commercial examples were produced over a century ago. (The American inventor, Hiram Maxim, was marketing them as early as 1902, and took out the first patent in 1908.) The term 'silencer' is also sometimes used, although this has fallen out of favour largely because of the gangster image promoted by popular fiction and movies.

Of course 'silencer' is also an inaccurate term, as it is impossible to truly silence a high velocity bullet. Servicemen may recall the 'crack and thump' demonstration, in which a round is fired over the heads of soldiers under training, to enable them to understand the theory of locating an enemy by his fire. When a rifle is fired, two sounds are actually heard if you are standing close to the passage of the bullet: the first is the supersonic 'crack' of the bullet passing, followed by the 'thump' of the rifle that follows shortly afterwards. It is the latter that gives away the direction of the firer, and the space between the two sounds also gives the observer a good indication of how far away the firer is. There is no doubt that deer, like other wildlife, are able to correlate the noises to determine the danger source.

Although sporting rifle moderators are classified as Section 1 firearms, it has never been easier to get one added to your Firearms Certificate. Not so long ago, firearms licensing departments were unwilling to grant such an addition to an FAC but now the situation is very different. Health and safety concerns, along with an increasing awareness of noise pollution, have played a large part in this, along with the potential for compensation claims arising from hearing loss. Interestingly, the sale of moderators remains unrestricted if for use with any air weapon that does not require an FAC.

The science involved in moderating a rifle is fairly simple. The gases produced by the fired cartridge are vented through a series of baffles, which cool and condense them before releasing them into the atmosphere; this reduces the noise of the final venting and thus the 'signature' of the rifle being fired (the 'thump'). It does not, of course, reduce the 'crack' of the bullet, nor indeed does it have any significant effect on velocity.

In terms of noise, fitting a moderator to a rifle can bring about a dramatic reduction. An unmoderated rifle produces over 160 decibels (dB) of sound, often considerably more depending on the rifle and calibre in use; adding a moderator can reduce this to as low as 130dB. For comparison, normal conversation is rated at around 60dB, a vacuum cleaner is about 70dB, and a chainsaw some 115dB. Under the EU Noise Directive, workers must be provided with ear defenders if noise levels in the work place exceed 80dB – if they reach 85dB, the wearing of ear defenders becomes compulsory.

If workers are subjected to impulsive noise, such as a gunshot, of more than 137dB, the Directive demands that the noise must be reduced at the point of origin in the most effective and technically possible way. Many employers, such as the Forestry Commission, and self-employed people bound by these regulations looked immediately to sound moderators as a means of complying.

Common sense demands that recreational users should do so as well, even if they are not subject to such stringent rules. After all, hearing damage is irreversible, and how many of us pause to put on hearing protection before taking a shot when we are not on the rifle range? Here immediately lies one of the most compelling arguments for moderating your rifle.

Noise suppression apart, there is any number of other benefits that come from fitting a moderator to your rifle. Recoil reduces by about a third (some manufacturers claim even more than that) and, perhaps as a consequence, most firers find that their shooting accuracy improves considerably. Muzzle flip also reduces, which means that the firer can watch the strike of the bullet or the reaction of the target.

All of these advantages mean that sound moderation is good for the environment, the stalker, and indeed the quarry. Disturbance to the environment, caused by the rolling booms of unmoderated gunshots, is minimised, and everything in the neighbourhood is not immediately put onto the alert by the first shot. The result is more effective and efficient stalking, with an increase in chances for the stalker. Furthermore, you are not waking up householders several fields away, nor causing unnecessary alarm. Noise nuisance in an ever-present consideration in the modern world, and the thinking stalker should always be mindful of means by which it can be reduced.

Disturbance to the environment is an interesting area, especially when you consider the effects of the moderated shot. Thinking back to the 'crack and thump' effect of the rifle, the deer certainly seem to have little idea of where the firer is located once the 'thump' is removed. Very often, when one out of a group falls, the remainder will actually move towards the firer – especially useful where there is a cull to complete. Interestingly, some park herd managers do not like to use moderators for this very reason, preferring the deer to know where the danger is coming from and when it has ceased. This allows them to settle more quickly once culling operations are over. An alternative point of view came to me from the manager of a large deer park in Europe, who shoots unmoderated for a totally different reason – he wants the general public to know that shooting is going on, and thus keep away!

As far as the deer are concerned, an increase in accuracy translates into more humane culling. Even if the shot is misplaced, the firer has a better chance of seeing what has gone wrong and planning an appropriate follow-up. Admittedly, there are a few disadvantages associated with moderating a rifle. Not least is the weight penalty of adding between 500 and 750 grams onto the muzzle end, with a corresponding change in balance; it is likely that a stalker who covers large distances on, say, the Scottish hill might find this unacceptable. You are also adding length to the rifle, although many moderator designs do sleeve back over the barrel and minimise this effect.

Owners of cherished rifles may well be unwilling to tamper with them, as there is no denying that a moderator changes the aesthetics considerably. Indeed, if there is a foresight present, this may well have to be removed to permit screw cutting or the fitting of some sleeve-back designs. However who, these days, chooses to shoot over iron sights? Screw cutting, it must be added, needs to be performed by a competent gunsmith to ensure that the thread of the moderator is properly matched and that all tolerances are correct. It is certainly not a job to be undertaken on a lathe at home.

Some countries, by the way, regulate the ownership or use of moderators in a totally different way to that of the UK, and some still ban their use completely. If you plan to use a moderated rifle for hunting abroad, it is worth checking local regulations first.

There is no need to be put off by the cost, which can be anything between £150 and £300 depending on the model you decide upon. Fitting may be extra, but these days new rifles are often supplied already screw-cut in the factory; if not, any competent gunsmith can do the job for you.

If you have not already taken the plunge and tried a moderator, I urge you to take the advice of a complete convert and have one fitted. You will notice the differences immediately and probably wonder, like me, why you didn't fit one years ago. Your shooting is likely to improve dramatically, and, as I have said, the environment will suffer less disturbance whenever you use it.

Above all your hearing, that most precious of commodities, will be protected. I cannot stress enough that hearing loss is irreversible. There is no excuse for the modern generation of stalkers to suffer it, now that such an integral form of protection is so readily available.

Some tips for moderator users

- If you are buying a new rifle/moderator combination, a shorter barrel reduces overall length and makes for a better balanced outfit.
- Take care that the thread on the moderator matches that on the muzzle end of the barrel, and that the calibre matches that of the rifle.
- Any plastic bushings on sleeve-back models must be drilled carefully to fit your individual rifle barrel properly – beware them being too loose.

- Ensure that the moderator is fully screwed hand-tight onto the barrel before firing, but take care not to over-tighten. A loose moderator may mean that your rifle shoots to a different point of impact.
- A new moderator may take a few shots to bed in, and it is always worth checking that it remains secure between strings of shots.
- Always remove the moderator from the rifle before storage to avoid any danger of the two being stuck together by chemical action. Unlike some of the older models of .22 moderators, zero will not alter between removal and refitting.
- If the moderator will not unscrew, try soaking the connection in easing oil. If you still cannot unscrew the moderator by hand, don't force the issue – a trip to the gunsmith is recommended.
- A quick spray of a suitable oil (such as WD40 or Napier) inside the moderator after firing neutralises any acidic deposits and prevents corrosion.
- Some manufacturers do not recommend stripping moderators for cleaning, or deep cleaning using ultrasonic baths to loosen deposits, because of the toxicity of these deposits and associated health and safety concerns.
- Some moderators are made of bright metal; a neoprene or rubber cover provides camouflage, prevents unnecessary noise, and will not affect zero.

MUNTJAC – A DEER FOR ALL SEASONS

The muntjac is a very primitive form of deer, which has evolved little over at least the last fifteen million years. It is a small prey species to which rapid reproduction is important; furthermore it originates from subtropical areas where the changing of the seasons are less marked. As such, it is unsurprising that breeding is not linked to specific times of the year. Furthermore, compared to other deer species, muntjac antlers are relatively simple and are a less significant factor in establishing breeding dominance over other bucks, whereas their canine teeth play an important part in disputes. A broken canine can seriously affect the buck's ability to dominate his rivals.

Generally speaking, the breeding cycles of the antlered species of deer are linked to the length of daylight hours, as this stimulates the female deer coming into oestrus, and promotes the production of the hormone testosterone in the males. As levels of the latter increase in the male deer, antler growth is stimulated, and conversely as they wane the reduced testosterone levels stimulate antler casting.

Mature muntjac bucks in their native China cast their antlers in May and have regrown and cleaned them again by September, very much as they do in this country.

Unlike most other deer, though, the muntjac remains sexually active all year round with no notable variation in the quantity and quality of their spermatozoa. Recent studies in China suggest that, in the muntjac, the threshold levels of testosterone needed for developing antlers are set higher than those required for the production of sperm and thus the male remains fertile throughout the year. The muntjac doe, having had her fawn, will not wait for a specific time to come into oestrus but instead comes into breeding condition almost immediately.

I ask people why they have deer heads on their walls. They always say because it's such a beautiful animal. There you go. I think my mother is attractive, but I have photographs of her. **Ellen DeGeneres**

MUNTJAC IN THE UK

Records indicate that London Zoo first exhibited Indian muntjac in 1829 and Reeves' (also known as Chinese) muntjac in 1838. The first animals arrived at Woburn in Bedfordshire, where they were confined to the deer park, during the 1890s. There is no evidence that either were truly present in the wild until 1901 when thirty-one Indian and eleven Reeves' muntjac were released in the vicinity of the park. The Indian animals appear to have died out fairly quickly, but the small population of Reeves' remained. Although Woburn is often cited as the epicentre of muntjac spread in our country, it was by no means the only collection to possess them and the wild population was certainly supplemented by releases and escapes from other collections in subsequent decades. Deliberate releases took place further afield during the 1930s and then again during the post-war years.

For a long time it was felt by many observers that British muntjac were a hybrid of the Indian and the Reeves'. Although the two species have been known to hybridise in captivity, none of the offspring have been fertile. Studies of chromosome structures have conclusively confirmed that the muntjac found in Britain is the Reeves'.

Initially numbers grew slowly. There were estimated to be only about four thousand muntjac in the wild by 1965, largely confined to the Midlands, but thereafter the population increased rapidly. Figures published by the Parliamentary Office of Science and Technology in 2009 suggest that UK numbers have reached over 150,000, and muntjac are certainly now widely distributed across much of England and Wales.

Further deliberate translocations have assisted this rapid spread, though the Wildlife and Countryside Act 1981 has since prohibited the unlicensed release of muntjac into the wild. A glance at distribution maps for muntjac in Britain will indicate small colonies well away from main populations, a sure sign of probable human assistance. The latter has doubtless been responsible for their recently recorded presence in Northern Ireland, and it has also been suggested they may be present in some parts of Scotland as well.

You might as well learn that a man who catches fish or shoots game has got to make it fit to eat before he sleeps. Otherwise it's all a waste and a sin to take it if you can't use it. **Robert Ruark, The Old Man and the Boy**

NOTIFIABLE DISEASES

Certain diseases carried by animals must be notified to the authorities so that they can be controlled and, where possible, eradicated. This is a legal requirement under the Animal Health Act 1981, which states that 'any person having in their possession or under their charge an animal affected or suspected of having one of these diseases must, with all practicable speed, notify that fact to a police constable'. Rather than doing that, it has become best practice that any occurrence is notified to the nearest branch of the Animal & Plant Health Agency (APHA), which was formed in October 2014 by merging the Animal Health and Veterinary Laboratories Agency (AHVLA) with parts of the Food and Environment Research Agency (FERA). APHA is responsible for investigating all incidents of suspected notifiable disease, amongst many other functions concerning animal, plant and bee health.

Notifiable diseases may be classified as exotic (not usually found in Britain), or endemic (normally present here). Up-to-date lists of both types can be found on the APHA and Defra websites. The two sites also give dates when a specific disease was last noted in this country. In addition the Defra site usefully lists which diseases are considered exotic and which endemic, and, very importantly, whether or not they are zoonotic (i.e. the disease can pass between animals and humans).

As far as deer are concerned, the main notifiable diseases are anthrax, bovine tuberculosis, bluetongue virus and foot-and-mouth disease, but there are many others and it is important that anyone who has an involvement with deer learns to recognise the signs of possible infection. Interestingly, warble fly, technically a parasite and not a disease, is also named. Many of the diseases identified have never actually occurred in Britain whilst others have not done so in living memory. Rinderpest, for example, was last recorded here in 1877 but is still listed.

If you find a dead deer, or examine a shot one, which you suspect may be infected with a notifiable disease, you should contact your local APHA office (contact details are listed on their website) who will instruct you on the next steps.

POINT BLANK RANGE

The term 'point blank' is much misunderstood. In popular fiction the phrase is often used to describe a situation where the barrel of the gun is almost touching the target. Correctly applied to ballistics, however, the term means something very different.

A bullet leaving a barrel, generally speaking, rises initially in relation to the line of sight but then travels in a falling curve (the trajectory) as gravity and other forces pull it towards earth and slow it down. If you want the bullet to strike a specific point on the target, it follows that you must aim off to allow for this when you are shooting at distances other than the one to which you have adjusted your sights.

Sometimes a target is not a specific point but a more general zone; in deer stalking, for example, we may want simply to ensure that the bullet strikes somewhere within a designated vital target area. In these circumstances we are interested in determining the distance between the firearm and the target and where the bullet will strike within that area without having to adjust the elevation of the firearm, instead still aiming at a central point on the target. This distance is the *point blank range*. The simple diagram below illustrates this:

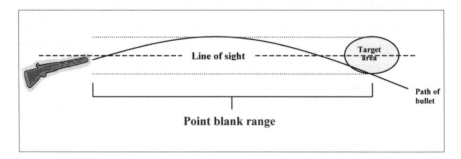

A firearm with a flatter trajectory will extend point blank range beyond that of one firing a slower or heavier bullet, which will start to decelerate and fall to earth more quickly. Some stalkers seek to extend the point blank range by zeroing their rifle so that the shots fall slightly high of the point of aim at a set distance, normally around 100 metres.

RANGEFINDERS

A rangefinder is a device that measures the distance between the observer and a chosen object. Nearly all of those currently available use a light beam, which bounces off the object and returns to the hand-held unit, enabling the time taken for this to happen to be measured and the range calculated accordingly. The reflectivity of various targets will affect the ability of the beam to do this – a 'hard' target, such as a large rock, has more reflectivity than a softer one, which will not reflect so well. Any obstructions between you and the object, as well as weather conditions, may also affect the efficiency of the beam. As long as the unit is able to obtain a reading, you should expect the accuracy to be in the region of plus or minus one metre.

The capability of the model you choose will almost inevitably be reflected in the price. Ultimately, what you pay will depend on the depth of your wallet and what you feel you need: costs can range from less than £100 for a budget model up to several thousand pounds for a top-of-the-range device. It is even possible to purchase binoculars with a rangefinder built in.

As most woodland stalkers seldom take a shot at much more than 100 metres it might be argued that a rangefinder is unnecessary – for if you are capable of judging reasonable shooting distances with the naked eye you should be more than capable of an acceptable level of accuracy. On the open hill, however, longer shots are often the norm, and some degree of 'holdover' will be required to allow for bullet drop as the range increases. Likewise, a rangefinder is immensely useful for determining ranges to given objects when in a fixed position (such as a high seat), so that valuable time is not wasted when a fleeting opportunity presents itself or to predetermine maximum shooting distances. Rangefinders can also be very helpful when setting out impromptu zeroing targets in the field.

There's an irresponsible owner behind every gun accident. **Maverick Saenz**

Danish Interlude

Not so long ago I travelled to Denmark to deliver a Deer Stalking Certificate 1 course to a group of gamekeeping students at the *Danmarks Jægerforbund*, or Danish Hunters Association, which runs a year-long Wildlife Management course at their school in Kalø on the east coast of Jutland. The students undergoing the course at the time had asked if they could take the DSC1 as many wanted to go on to work, or at least stalk, in the UK.

On the range day the rolling crash of multiple rifles came as something of a surprise after UK conditions. At the time Danish law did not permit the use of moderators with hunting rifles. The noise was accentuated by the fact that the Danes are fond of larger calibres as their deer, particularly the reds, can be big. I was very glad of a good pair of ear defenders. 'Would you like to show us how it's done?' asked Nicholai, our range officer for the day, as he offered me the choice between a .223 and a lightly built .300 Winchester Magnum, with a mischievous grin. Honour demanded that I had to choose the Win Mag.

You don't seem to notice the recoil of an unmoderated rifle when you are in a real shooting situation, but concentrating intently on a zeroing target on a rifle range it's rather different, especially with such an unforgiving calibre. I was acutely aware of the kick hammering into my shoulder and, worse, my brain seemed to rattle inside its casing with every shot.

Miraculously I achieved a decent group and moved on to the deer target which I also managed to complete successfully.

It's a good job that I did; I had developed such a flinch by the end that I certainly wouldn't have managed a second attempt. As I recovered from the punishment I found myself wishing the Danes good fortune for a change in the law regarding moderators, which I'm pleased to say they received in 2014.

RED DEER ANTLERS

A mature red stag will generally cast his antlers in March or April and regrow them over the summer, being clean of velvet by August or September. This means that in reality the period of growth lasts some twelve to sixteen weeks, although this is dependent on the habitat and availability of food. It is widely accepted that the red deer of East Anglia are some of the largest to be found in Britain, living in an environment that gives them all that they could wish for in terms of forage, cover and climate. They consequently develop higher body weights and larger antlers than their brethren who live in the poorer conditions offered by the Scottish hill. Antler development is also faster there than it is in Scotland; those produced by a two-year-old East Anglian stag might be comparable to a Highland four- or five-year-old. It is extremely rare for a Scottish stag to produce antlers to rival those of their southern counterparts.

A good Norfolk stag might grow antlers with a main beam of some 90 centimetres, with the additional points making up a further 140 centimetres. This means that there might be as much as 230 centimetres or more of overall growth involved. Applying an average time of 14 weeks or 98 days required to produce this single antler, it follows that a growth rate of one inch or 2.5 centimetres a day is not unreasonable. This is just for one antler of course – the stag is in fact producing two simultaneously, so one inch a day might be only a conservative estimate. Such prodigious antler growth can clearly only be achieved where the very best resources are available to the animal.

REINDEER OR CARIBOU?

The two animals are one and the same; the name given simply depends on where they come from. Caribou, a French Canadian word, is more usually applied to the North American reindeer. There are nine sub-species of *Rangifer tarandus* occurring naturally across northern Europe, Siberia and North America. A domesticated form also exists and has been successfully introduced to places as far afield as South Georgia and China.

Although there are wide variations between the sub-species, a typical male reindeer can measure anything between 40 and 47 inches high at the shoulders, with a full grown North American bull caribou reaching as high as 50 inches and weighing up to 600 pounds. They are fascinating deer in many ways; the large hooves are designed for travelling over soft snow or boggy ground and, unlike other deer, the nose is completely covered by short, soft hairs, which protect against frostbite. Even their nasal bones are specially adapted to give a larger surface to warm the incoming cold air and extract moisture from it. One particular characteristic of the species is the clicking sound made by their foot tendons when walking: this allows the herd to stay in contact at night or in adverse weather conditions. Unique among deer, both males and females grow antlers. Reindeer moss, a lichen, forms a major part of their winter diet.

Wild reindeer existed in Scotland until about the tenth century when they finally died out. Although there are reindeer in Britain today they are not truly wild. In 1952 a herd was established at Rothiemurchus and animals there are allowed to range freely in the Cairngorms when not in their fenced enclosure. The herd is now about 150 strong. A few are kept at the Glenmore visitor centre, about six miles to the east of Aviemore, and trips are available to visit the main herd on the mountain-side where, with an experienced guide, you can walk amongst the deer.

The rifle itself has no moral stature, since it has no will of its own. **Jeff Cooper,** *Art of the Rifle*

SENSITIVE ANTLERS

Early one March I received a query from someone who had been watching a particular group of roe from her house. An older buck had occasionally shown dominance towards a younger one by prodding it with its antlers, and on the morning in question the two older bucks in the group actually sparred with their antlers, which were still in velvet. As growing antlers consist of living tissue, complete with a blood supply, they are very sensitive and a deer will usually take great care to avoid letting them make contact with anything. How, then, was this possible?

The older bucks in the group under observation may have cast their antlers as early as last October, while the younger ones might not have done so until as late as early December. New antlers begin to regrow almost immediately, and it takes over three months for the process to complete. Throughout this time, the antlers are covered in the furry covering known as velvet. As the growth cycle ends, the blood supply to the living bone and velvet is cut off and the new antler effectively becomes inert bone itself, though attached to the living bone of the skull. The velvet dies and is eventually rubbed off by the buck through fraying.

By early March, the old bucks in the group would probably have reached the stage when they were ready to clean the velvet from their antlers, which had finished developing although still covered by velvet. As such, they would have consisted of what is essentially dead bone and lost their sensitivity, so it would have caused the bucks no discomfort to spar with them. Any younger bucks in the group, however, would still have had an amount of growth to complete, and in fact it is not unusual to see young bucks still in velvet during May or even into June. By contrast, some older bucks have actually been seen in hard horn as early as late February. This head start gives them an important dominance at a time of year when they want to establish their territories during the spring.

Clarissa

I first met the late television cook and countryside campaigner, Clarissa Dickson Wright, when I was called over by a mutual friend to be introduced to her at a game fair. 'Charles is writing a book about muntjac deer', Sally told her.

The larger-than-life lady regarded me shrewdly for a moment before speaking. 'They've got frightfully long tongues, haven't they?' she eventually asked.

I said that, yes, for their small size, they have got quite long tongues. 'Can you get me some?' came the request.

What on earth, I had to ask, did she want them for? 'To cook, you stupid boy' was the reply.

I was already at an age when being called a stupid boy caused no offence, although I quickly learned that Clarissa had no qualms about what she said to anybody. We chatted for a while and I realised that here was a highly intelligent, quick, warm and witty person hidden behind a gruff exterior. Before we parted to go our separate ways I promised to collect some tongues for her.

For the next few months I kept the tongue of every muntjac I shot, wrapping each one carefully in clingfilm and adding it to a large freezer bag labelled clearly 'Tongues for Clarissa'. My long-suffering wife came to terms with this eventually. I finally decided to call it a day when I was at the deer larder of a well known local estate on a moved cull day, and was unkindly described as performing 'Charles's Burke-and-Hare routine' on the assembled muntjac carcases. Enough was enough, and the freezer bag was duly dropped off with Sally for Clarissa to pick up next time she was in the area.

The tongues were, apparently, delicious, fried in butter with salt and pepper, although I've never really felt the urge to try them myself. Clarissa thanked me profusely the next time we met, accompanying the thanks with a large hug. It was like being attacked by a she-bear.

Clarissa's death in 2014 robbed the countryside of one of its most staunch and outspoken supporters. She was fearless of controversy and never ducked doing what she felt to be the right thing, even if it brought her onto the wrong side of the law. Her passion, outspokenness and enthusiasm for the countryside will be sorely missed 'at the barricades', as she liked to put it.

SIKA – THE ROBUST DEER

For my money, our non-native sika and muntjac are the most robust deer when it comes to shooting. Of course all deer will succumb quickly to a properly placed bullet from a legal calibre, but these two species seem to have a more highly developed flight reflex, and will often do surprising things once hit.

Sika, though, have a real reputation amongst experienced stalkers for their hardiness. One of my earliest experiences with this species came down in Dorset when I was accompanying a very experienced sika stalker on an evening outing. It was the time of the rut, and we found a large group of frustrated prickets who were keeping a wary distance from a dominant stag. We edged into position in a ditch and Terry pointed out an animal on the edge of the group as my target. At around a hundred yards it was a simple shot with the .243 and the animal jumped, took a couple of paces and dropped to a heart shot. As I chambered a fresh round the group milled about, unsure of where the shot had come from, and I was instructed to take another.

Another pricket stood broadside and the .243 barked again. The shot felt good, but, rather than falling, my target merely shook itself. There was no lurch, jump or blundering run: instead the deer started to amble towards the dense gorse along the edge of the field as though it didn't have a care in the world. It was getting dark and Terry was not prepared to take the chance of a potentially long search in the thick cover, so he shot it again with his 30-06 and the animal went down. (He told me later that he had seen similar reactions to shot before, which had resulted in some very long and occasionally fruitless searches.) The little 100 grain bullet from my rifle had taken the top off the sika's heart but, with a body full of adrenaline, it was simply not going to accept that it was dead until it had to. Terry's bigger 30-06 bullet was only really necessary to drop the beast but without it the deer could have gone hundreds of yards before falling, with the very real danger under the circumstances of a lost carcase.

On another occasion a friend, once again using a .243, shot a good sika stag at a range of almost 200 yards. At the shot the animal jumped and ran, but the professional stalker accompanying her was not concerned as there was plenty of encouraging blood sign indicating a mortal hit. After handshakes and congratulations all round, the group set off to recover the beast, following a strong blood trail which eventually ran out. An hour later, dejected and dispirited, they were forced by darkness to abandon the search.

The carcase was recovered at first light the next morning with the assistance of a good dog, which tracked the animal's final rush for some 300 yards before finding it, its antlers entangled in a juniper bush. It had taken this distance before the stag, although clinically dead for most of it, actually fell.

It is all a question of terminal energy. Although there will be variations depending on factors such as bullet design and cartridge load, a little 100 grain .243 bullet, travelling at some 2,500 feet per second at 100 yards, might produce around 1,650 foot pounds of energy dropping to 1,400 foot pounds at 200 yards. Compare that with a slower .308 150 grain bullet, which gives 2,200 and 1,800 foot pounds respectively at the same ranges. In layman's terms, this translates into greater 'knock down' power which will cause the deer to fall on the spot rather than take off in an automatic flight reflex, literally running dead on its feet.

We all have our favourite calibres. I still like to use my .243 for roe and smaller, but for larger deer tend to reach for the .308. On the open hill it doesn't matter so much if a stag runs before dropping as you can observe its progress, but in close country having good 'knock down' can often mean the difference between finding a deer where it was hit and a long search – and with sika especially I think that it is vital.

SITING YOUR HIGH SEAT

SOME TIPS ON HOW TO GET THE BEST OUT OF YOUR HIGH SEATS

March has always been the traditional time for stalkers to get on with all of those little jobs that have been on hold until now. The woods are still fairly bare of new growth, and hopefully you have the cull completed or at least under control. It's quite likely that you will have identified a few good spots over the winter and are thinking about putting up a new high seat or two. It pays to take care when selecting new seat locations as it's easy to waste a great deal of time, effort and money putting up a permanent construction if you get it wrong. The first important question is – do the deer actually use the area? If you know your ground well you should have the answer, but beware that movement patterns can change from time to time and are especially affected by weather and land disturbance.

You also need to consider longer-term land usage before putting up a permanent seat. The chosen site may be good for now, but are any changes to the woodland or agricultural use going to move the deer elsewhere or put a seat out of action in some other way? Beware especially of young plantations; I know of two elaborate box seats, erected to protect new plantings, which were rendered useless within a short time as the growing trees eliminated views of the ground in all directions. They still stand in the middle of these plantations, surrounded by trees that have now grown to match their height, as a testament to short-sighted planning.

Portable seats are a very useful solution to short-term problems, and as a way of proving a site worthy of a full-time structure. They are quick and simple to erect, but do take care in areas where there is public access. Being easily carried they are just as easy to steal, so make sure that they are secured to their supporting tree by a stout chain and padlock to deter the opportunist thief. These days, I'm afraid, cordless cutting equipment can make short work of even the strongest chain so don't leave them in the same position for too long.

If you have identified a clearing or small field which attracts regular visits by deer, it's time to start thinking about where the best place for the seat is going to be. If it's a lean-to type, you'll need a suitable tree to which you can secure it. This needs to be large enough to prevent the seat from swaying in the wind, and sufficiently clear of branches to allow visibility from it. You also want sufficient background to break up or disguise your silhouette.

Whilst good fields of fire are important, don't look for big, uninterrupted vistas for hundreds of yards in every direction. Such places will discourage deer, which may feel too exposed and uncomfortable to want to hang around in them for long. Small glades or scallops in a woodline are much better than wide open spaces; preferably choose a view with plenty of scattered cover, as this not only offers browsing opportunities to attract the deer out but also allows them to relax. It doesn't matter if a deer is temporarily out of your view, as it will eventually move into a position offering you a shot. By the same token you don't need to be able to see for hundreds of yards; restrict yourself to places where whatever you see will be within a realistic range for a shot. In practical terms this needs to be no more than about 150 yards, depending on a realistic appraisal of the competence of those you expect to be doing the shooting. What's the point of offering the temptation of long, risky shots? Always make sure that there are safe backstops for the bullet when anyone does get a chance.

Try to identify regular movement lines which are worth overlooking. You will often find well-used deer paths, or racks, which give away the habitual routes that deer take between their feeding and bedding areas. Hedge lines or other sources of cover in more open areas are well worth paying attention to as well. If overlooking a ride or a track, try to site the seat at a junction where you have views in more than one direction. If the undergrowth is thick among the trees, tracks are probably the only opportunity open to you within a wood actually to see deer as they move about. Wider rides with vegetation on each side may persuade the deer to linger rather than cross without stopping. If your ground holds a pheasant shoot, the deer will learn to visit the feeders, especially when natural forage is sparse during the winter, so having one or two of these within range of your seat can pay dividends. In the same way, game crops can also be productive.

When putting up the seat, angle it in such a way that your firing position will be as comfortable as possible in every direction. Right-handed shooters will find shots to their extreme right awkward and vice versa. Try instead to set the seat at an angle to your main shooting direction that suits you. If both left- and right-handed shooters will be using it, straight ahead is the best compromise. Do take care to avoid places where people may approach unseen, such as footpaths or other public areas.

Don't forget to provide yourself with a suitable approach route, preferably into the prevailing wind direction for your ground. If you fill the ground in front of the seat with your scent you will give the game away before you even occupy it. An alternative route in for when the wind direction changes is also helpful. Keep your approach clear of new growth so that you can move into position silently, and don't cut the path in a straight line; put a dog leg in it so that you are not in full view of the area you plan to overlook as you walk in.

Some kind of range marking is especially useful in more enclosed areas where shooting chances may be fleeting. You may not have time to check with a rangefinder, and in poor light it is quite easy to mistake the range to your target. I have seen white-topped range posts set out at fifty-yard intervals, or even the actual range painted onto the sides of trees, but different coloured splashes of paint on tree trunks and other available objects are just as effective as long as the observer knows the colour code. Alternately, you can fix range cards onto the rails of your seats – just laminate a few blank copies and complete them in permanent marker pen.

Finally, don't forget your extraction route if you have a carcase. It is one thing packing out a roe or a muntjac, but a bigger deer can be very awkward if you can't get to it with the Land Rover or quad bike.

The dog is a gentleman; I hope to go to his heaven not man's. **Mark Twain**

ST HUBERT

The story of St Hubert, or Hubertus, originates in seventh century Belgium. Like other young noblemen of his time, Hubert was an accomplished huntsman who withdrew from court life following the death of his wife in childbirth and moved to the forests of the Ardennes to devote himself to the chase.

One day, when he was in pursuit of a magnificent white stag, the animal suddenly turned and Hubert saw a vision of a gleaming crucifix between its antlers. At the same time he heard a voice, which told him to cease his hunting and instead lead a more devout life by seeking out Bishop Lambert of Maastricht and putting himself under this cleric's instruction. Hubert obediently did not shoot at the stag and did as he was directed. He renounced his nobility, distributed his wealth among the poor and was ordained a priest. He eventually became Bishop of Maastricht himself, and later the first Bishop of Liège.

Hubert died in the year AD 727 and was buried in the Church of St Peter in Liège, although his bones were exhumed about a hundred years later and transferred to the Benedictine Abbey of Amdain, in modern-day

Saint-Hubert. The Abbey became an important destination for pilgrims until the saint's remains, by then consisting of just two thigh bones, were lost during the Reformation. Hubert had been consecrated as a saint in AD 743 but his feast day, 3rd November, is believed to be the date of the transfer of his remains to Amdain. He is remembered as the 'Apostle of the Ardennes'.

Saint Hubert Clubs for hunters exist all over the world, including in Britain, whilst the Saint Hubert hound is the forerunner of the modern bloodhound. As well as being the patron saint of hunters, Hubert also protects archers, dogs, forest workers, mathematicians, metal workers, opticians and trappers. He was venerated across medieval Europe, even to the point that his name was widely invoked as a cure for rabies. Thanks partly to his noble birth, several chivalric orders were also named for him. There is a chapel dedicated to St Hubert in the Ardennes, close to where his vision of the stag is said to have taken place, and also one in Idsworth, Hampshire.

STALKING KIT

WHAT'S IN YOUR ROE SACK?
MAYBE IT'S TIME TO GET BACK TO BASICS...

How many of us carry a selection of stalking items that we never seem to use? A recent clear-out of my field kit brought to light any number of odd pieces of equipment which seemed a good idea at the time, but were now no more than dead weight that I was simply lugging around for no good reason. Admittedly, what one needs to carry is often determined by local circumstances, but perhaps now is a good time to take a hard look at our stalking kit and decide what is – and isn't – really necessary.

To be honest, many of us have moved away from the roe sack and taken to wearing a waist-belt, or bum bag, these days. The sack remains very useful when you need to carry a dead roe or muntjac a long distance, but on my main stalking grounds you are never that far away from a track. Fewer pockets, as well, mean that there is less tempting space to fill up with clutter.

THE ESSENTIALS

Apart from rifle and ammunition, there is not very much else that you can classify as truly essential. Do take enough ammunition though; even if you are only expecting to shoot one or two deer, there is always the possibility that something might go wrong and you will need more. For the sake of a full magazine, plus another or a spare pouch in your pocket, you will have plenty to fall back on if necessary, or if you find yourself having one of those rare red-letter days.

Don't forget your FAC either; if challenged, the law requires that you must prove your right to be out and about with a rifle.

I would also consider a pair of binoculars to be essential stalking items. True, you will have a scope on the rifle, but you don't want to be waving that about when scanning your surroundings. A suitable stalking stick is also important; there's never a convenient tree when you need to take a standing shot. Add a sharp knife to the ensemble and you really do have the basic equipment needed to find, shoot and deal with a deer.

VERY USEFUL – 'GOOD TO HAVE'

It's never as simple as that, of course, and that is why I find that pockets alone don't provide enough storage space, hence the need for a bum bag. To gralloch a deer efficiently and hygienically in the field you require a bit more than just a knife. A small bone saw makes short work of the breast and pelvic bone, and saves the edge on your knife. A handful of disposable rubber gloves allows you to keep your hands clean (there's never water to hand when you need it) and of course to save cross-contamination if you need to change them during the gralloch. A couple of plastic bags are useful in which to keep liver, kidneys, heart and anything you plan to boil up as dog food. Finally, a couple of S hooks are a great help if you are going to suspend a carcase from a branch when gralloching or to cool afterwards.

I'd also consider some form of signalling device as important. Even in the south of England you may find yourself a long way from help in an emergency. Mobile telephones are useful, but you cannot always rely on having a good signal. It's no use finding out that there isn't one when you are lying at the bottom of a high seat with a broken leg. Consider a radio, a good quality whistle or a pre-arranged sequence of shots. If everyone is using moderators, it will be clear that something is wrong if two or three unmoderated shots sound in the woods.

If you are stalking during the evening, a good torch not only provides light for working in the dark, but also for searching for a lost deer if necessary. The sort that you can wear on your head allows you to have both hands free when gralloching, or when carrying your kit and a deer back to the car. A simple first-aid kit completes this part of the list. Work on the principle that if you've got one, you probably won't need it. If you are not carrying one, though...

Optional – 'nice to have'

Into the final category I tend to lump everything which is good to have to hand, but which I could live without at a pinch. A squeezable Buttolo roe call lives in its own pocket of the bum bag so that I can squeeze it in a hurry if I need to stop a muntjac or roe which is moving off; a short 'peep' on it usually halts a deer long enough to allow a shot. In the drink bottle pocket I keep a small foam mat for sitting on when in a high seat. The more comfortable you are, the less likely you are to fidget. I'll admit that I also carry a small pocket radio with earphone to stave off boredom when absolutely nothing seems to be moving in the woods.

I also carry a small rangefinder, mainly for predetermining ranges when I'm static in a seat or on a vantage point. This saves valuable time when a deer steps out of cover. It is surprising how easy it can be to misjudge ranges, especially in poor light. A small strobe light, designed to clip onto a dog's collar for night tracking, is also useful for marking the position of a carcase which you may have to return for later in the dark.

I've also always carried a spare knife, originally in case I'd forgotten to slip the sheath onto my belt, but now that the latter lives in the bum bag anyway it's still good to have two in case one loses its edge. An alternative, of course, is to carry a small sharpener or a stone. A packet of tissues often comes in handy in many ways, including cleaning up dirty blades after the deer has been dealt with and, torn into small pieces, for marking the progress of a blood trail if you have to follow up an animal.

IN THE CAR

A carcase tray in the car ensures that you can get your deer home clean and without covering everything in blood; a small piece of lining material (poncho sheets from the Army surplus supplier are excellent) can be used as an alternative. The car also provides a storage area for things that you might need but don't have to keep immediately to hand, such as a pruning saw to clear fire lanes around high seats, carcase tags, or a hand pulley and gambrel for dealing with larger carcases.

The list that I've provided is not exhaustive, and of course each person will have his or her own preferences and priorities. I stress that my list really covers woodland stalking; if you are operating in remote or inhospitable terrain you may have to look harder at what you carry, especially with emergencies or carcase extraction in mind. I do also carry a small Silva compass which almost certainly saved my life once, but that's another story for another day.

STALKING OPTICS

CONSIDERING THE CHOICES OPEN TO WOODLAND STALKERS

Choosing optics for woodland stalking often takes second place to purchasing a rifle, yet the opposite really ought to be the truth. Modern stalking rifles are capable of excellent accuracy, though it is impossible to make use of this if the scope on top of the firearm is not up to the job. Likewise, if your binoculars are incapable of spotting or clearly identifying the quarry, you probably won't even get into a position to consider a shot. In short, good optics can be the difference between success and failure.

I often think that deciding on what optics are best for you is similar to choosing a bottle of wine. You can pick up something very drinkable for a few pounds, or select a truly stunning vintage for over a hundred, but only you can make that value judgement as to whether the financial mark-up is worth it. It's the same with optics: choosing the right binoculars or riflescope is a delicate balance between what you want, what you need, and ultimately the depth of your pockets.

Because some of the most likely times for seeing wild deer are periods of low visibility, such as dawn or dusk, your optics must be able to use the available light as efficiently as possible. Binocular and scope specifications are given in two numbers, such as 8x42 or 7x50. The first figure is the magnification offered; the second is the size of the object lens in millimetres. If you divide the object lens by the magnification, you obtain a figure known as the exit pupil. For instance, a pair of 7x50 glasses will produce an exit pupil of just over 7mm. As the maximum aperture of the human eye is about 7mm under extreme low light conditions there is no point in exceeding this figure, but the closer the exit pupil is to it, the better the theoretical light-gathering capability of the glasses. In variable power scopes, the exit pupil will vary according to the magnification used in relation to the fixed size of the object lens.

In reality, the better the optical quality, the smaller the object lens you can get away with, saving on both size and weight. It's worth noting that a high quality set of 8x42 glasses can significantly outperform a cheap pair of 7x50s, so it pays to 'try before you buy', preferably in conditions of low light. I've always thought 7x42 ideal, but for some reason there does not seem to be the choice available in this combination that there used to be.

Ideally you need to match the quality of your binoculars to that of your rifle scope – what's the point, after all, of being able to see your target clearly with the former but not being able to pick it up through the latter? And do give a thought to weight; binoculars, especially, can become a heavy strain on the neck over the course of a long day's stalking.

Although the optical quality of binoculars and scopes has come a very long way in recent years, don't be tempted by cheaper rifle scopes intended for use with air rifles or rimfires. They are not designed to withstand the punishing recoil of a full bore, and will quickly lose their zero or, even worse, may even start to come apart. A good scope will hold its zero shot after shot.

It can be very tempting to choose a higher magnification than you need, but beware; the higher the magnification, the more any user-shake in either scope or binocular will be amplified. Most people find 8x a reasonable limit for handheld optics. Higher magnifications are of course easily stabilised by bipods or other rests, but the woodland stalker doesn't usually have these available. Although I have variable power scopes on my stalking rifles, these usually remain fixed at 6x, although I find it very useful to reduce the magnification occasionally where the cover is thick and any chances of a shot are likely to be at a very close range. It is very rare for me to use the full magnification available, and to be honest it's usually only on the rifle range.

With the hindsight of long stalking experience, during which I have used a wide variety of scopes and binoculars, the best general advice I can offer is to buy the very best that you can afford. Look on it as a long-term investment; quality means that you won't feel the need to upgrade in a year or two's time, and to top it all you'll see, and as a result shoot, more deer.

SUPPLEMENTARY FEEDING

Although supplementary feeding of deer is not generally practised in Britain, visitors to the Continent often notice that it is quite a widespread custom there. Many areas provide hay mangers, feed dispensers and mineral licks for the deer, usually to promote higher body weights or antler growth, or to improve the condition and subsequent breeding successes of hinds and does. Sometimes the aim is to support a higher deer population than would normally be possible for the ground in question, particularly if the land is under heavy hunting pressure.

In Britain, however, the more accepted management approach is to maintain deer numbers in balance with their natural environment, without any reliance on artificial feeding. Even in winter there is usually sufficient forage in the woods and on the hill to support the deer through the leaner months. Intensive feeding in the months leading up to winter allows the deer to lay down fat reserves which they can fall back upon when food is scarce. Long periods of snow and ice mean that, without available food, these reserves are quickly used up and it is then that the deer start to suffer.

At such times it might seem that providing artificial feed is the answer. Sadly, though, changes to a deer's diet have to be made very slowly as their stomachs – or more accurately, the specialised protozoan flora that exist in the rumen to ensure efficient digestion – cannot instantly adapt to any new foodstuffs. The process can take as long as two weeks. As a result it is possible for a starving deer fed something that it is not used to, such as hay, to die of malnutrition despite having a full stomach. Emergency feeding, regrettably, tends to come too late to have any positive effect.

The Emergency Knife

It had been a successful midwinter stalk but, too late, I discovered that I'd forgotten my knife. Now I found myself a mile or so from the car in the middle of Salisbury Plain with three roe does to deal with. I remembered a tip I'd read in a shooting magazine. Retrieving up one of the fired cases, I found two large stones and bashed the neck closed between them. The writer of the article had claimed that this would create a sufficient edge to perform as a blade in emergencies. Sadly it didn't, and it was hard, sweaty work getting the ungralloched carcases back to the car. I ended up dealing with them in our garden. Since that day I've always carried a spare knife.

SWIMMING DEER

L ike so many other land mammals, deer are capable of being very good swimmers if they need to be. The reindeer or caribou is especially proficient, aided by its specially adapted hooves, which are widely splayed for travelling over snow or boggy ground. These feet function as a very efficient way for the animal's propulsion through water; one observer claimed to have recorded a reindeer swimming at an average speed of two miles per hour, but as being capable of more than twice that speed if put under pressure. Another recorded that two men paddling a canoe only just managed to keep up with a swimming animal with very great difficulty. The hollow hairs of the reindeer's coat are also a great aid to buoyancy, and as a result they ride very high in the water. As a migratory species, reindeer will cross large bodies of water on a regular basis.

Other species are equally adept. The moose, or European elk, is very much at home in aquatic habitats and known to cross long stretches of water, often exceeding twenty kilometres, quite regularly. They will feed on submerged aquatic plants and have been seen to dive for plants in water deeper than five metres. One watcher noted that the animals are able to remain submerged for so long that no ripples show on the surface above the spot where they went down. Moose swim much lower in the water than reindeer and the rump is usually submerged.

All of the deer found in Britain have been known to swim. Red deer frequently cross Scottish lochs when searching for hinds during the rut, and fallow have a considerable reputation for using water as a route out of enclosures and hence establishing feral populations. Roe are not daunted by large bodies of water either, despite swimming almost completely submerged with only the head and neck showing. Occasionally they have been swept out to sea by strong currents, to be rescued by fishermen. Sika are well known for their ability in water; famously, when some were released onto Brownsea Island in 1896, where the intention was that the sea would contain them there, they promptly crossed Poole Harbour and established themselves on the Dorset mainland.

Muntjac have been seen deliberately entering ponds and lakes during pheasant shoots and concealing themselves under overhung banks until the disturbance has ended. Surprisingly, of all our deer, the Chinese water deer is the one that has been least seen actually in water!

You have to think about one shot. One shot is what it's all about. A deer has to be taken with one shot. I try to tell people that, they don't listen. **Robert De Niro as Michael in the film** *The Deer Hunter*

THE FALSE RUT

The roe rut is normally complete by the middle of August. It tends to start in late July and usually goes on for about three weeks. Due to delayed implantation, a particular feature of roe breeding behaviour, the fertilised egg does not start developing normally until December and the young are born in May or June.

In late September and in October roe bucks are occasionally seen behaving as though they are rutting, engaging in renewed barking and fraying, and questing along the tracks of does with their noses to the ground. It is most likely that the bucks in question are younger ones, as the older bucks are least likely to be still fertile at this time of the year. This is commonly known as the false rut.

Although it is highly unlikely that a roe doe would be fully receptive to the advances of a buck at this time, it would be dangerous to state this as an absolute. It has been suggested that the false rut may be a vestige of a time when roe rutted in the autumn before developing the ability for delayed implantation, or that the process might involve precocious fawns that have come into season late in the year: rare instances of roe fawn pregnancy have certainly been recorded. Whatever the case, many respected observers of deer have noted rutting behaviour and seen roe mating well into September and beyond.

TRIGGER DESIGN

Many shooters pay little attention to the design of the trigger on their rifle. On a shotgun, of course, this can be of lesser importance, but to the rifleman a correctly designed trigger is a vital aid to achieving real accuracy.

As far as shape is concerned, a wide variety of triggers can be found: these can range from those which are effectively straight, to more deeply curved 'match' triggers, which allow a more consistent pressure to be applied by the finger. Sporting rifles tend towards a compromise between the two. As the trigger is a mechanical device which releases the firing pin to strike the primer of the cartridge, the ease and regularity with which it does so is an essential factor in consistent and accurate shooting. When selecting a rifle, check that your finger can actually reach the trigger properly, rather than having to settle for a poor grip in order to do so.

The pressure at which the trigger is set to release the firing mechanism is also important. Theoretically, the less the pressure that is required, the more accurate you will be, but if too little pressure is needed it makes it easier to release a shot unintentionally with potentially dangerous consequences. For this reason some rifle manufacturers pre-set trigger pressures at a level which is too heavy and, when buying a new rifle, it is worth checking that the pressure can be adjusted to your personal requirements. Most sporting riflemen find that a trigger pressure of around three-and-a-half pounds is about right for them. Triggers can be single-stage or two-stage, the latter having a degree of slack that must be taken up before the rifle fires. The ideal let-off should be clean and crisp, often described as like breaking glass.

Take special care when using a set or hair trigger, which allows the trigger to be 'set' so that only the lightest touch is required to fire the rifle. Whilst set triggers certainly aid accurate shooting under the right conditions, they can also increase the risk of accidental discharge when crawling or otherwise moving with a rifle made ready to fire.

WHAT CALIBRE?

BEFORE BUYING A STALKING RIFLE YOU NEED TO DECIDE WHAT CALIBRE IT WILL BE

One good way to provoke an argument among experienced deer stalkers is to ask the question – what's the best calibre? Everyone has their favourite and I can guarantee that there will be little agreement. The only thing you can be certain of is that, once the dust settles, they will remain just as firmly entrenched in their personal preferences as they were at the start.

So what is the newcomer to deer stalking to choose? Far too many people seem to see a rifle that they like the look of and buy on that basis, only to find that it's not right for them. Others are influenced by what other stalkers recommend. Let's try to shed a little light on what seems, on the surface, to be a bewildering choice.

Firstly, it's important to get the legal side absolutely clear. To stalk all species of deer in England and Wales you'll need a calibre of at least .240 of an inch, generating a muzzle energy of at least 1,700 foot pounds. For muntjac and Chinese water deer the calibre and muzzle energy can drop to .220 of an inch and 1,000 foot pounds respectively, but the bullet weight will need to be at least 50 grains. In Scotland the requirements are slightly different and the actual calibre is not specified; for roe you'll need a 50 grain bullet with a muzzle velocity of 2,450 feet per second and a muzzle energy of at least 1,000 foot pounds. For larger deer the bullet size rises to 100 grains and the muzzle energy to 1,750 foot pounds. In Northern Ireland the law is again slightly different, requiring a calibre of at least .236 of an inch, a muzzle energy of 1,700 foot pounds or more and a bullet weight of at least 100 grains. If you are getting confused, there really is no need to be. For our purposes these laws mean that the smallest practical and widely available legal calibre for shooting any species of deer in the United Kingdom is the popular .243 Winchester, provided you are careful about the bullet you use with it. Some of the smaller bullet weights, which are very popular for vermin control, simply won't generate sufficient muzzle energy for deer.

If you opt for 100 grain bullets you should be well within the law; lower weights may also work but you would be well advised to test them on a rifle range using a chronograph first to ensure that they meet the legal minimum requirements. It's worth adding that any bullet used for shooting deer must be designed to deform in a predictable manner on striking the target, so full metal jackets are not a legal option.

In many ways the .243 is a perfect entry-level calibre for a beginner to full bore rifle shooting. It has low recoil, especially when teamed with a sound moderator, has a relatively flat trajectory and will cleanly kill any species of deer found in the UK. I have used the .243 through a variety of rifles for over thirty years and have found it perfectly satisfactory. Admittedly, it has a few minor drawbacks; as a relatively fast bullet it is capable of transmitting considerable hydrostatic shock as it passes through the deer and can cause disproportionate meat damage around the area of the strike. Curiously, a larger but slower bullet is less likely to produce such a wide radius of damage. Also, as a small calibre, the bullet sizes available commercially are restricted and the actual terminal energy transmitted when the bullet strikes the deer is limited. Although the deer, fairly struck, will be dead on its feet, it may be able to run a short way before falling. A larger bullet transfers more energy and you are more likely to drop the deer on the spot. On open ground this is not an issue, but in close woodland you may find that you have to search for your dead deer more carefully. The .243 may also not produce a sizeable exit wound on larger deer such as fallow, which means that you will have less of a blood trail to lead you to the carcase if necessary. A larger calibre offers you the option of larger bullets, and potentially a wider range of weights that you can use through your rifle. A glance at one major manufacturer's catalogue shows .243 ammunition available in weights ranging from 55 to 100 grains, of which only the upper end are of use to deer stalkers. The .308, on the other hand, is available in 125 to 220 grain loads, with 150 grains generally considered a good compromise for anything from muntjac to big red stags. This flexibility is of immense value in the future if you decide to go in search of larger quarry such as wild boar or African plains game. You also have greater versatility when it comes to bullet design, and of course there is the possibility (though hopefully a minor one) of restrictions on lead in bullets in the future. It's notoriously difficult to stabilise smaller bullets constructed from lighter materials, such as copper, in lighter weights.

Every now and then you read of a new sporting cartridge being developed. I'd advise a newcomer to steer clear of these no matter how enthusiastically these 'wildcats' are billed as the latest innovation in hunting calibres. You would be better off sticking to the tried and tested standards, many of which have been available for a long time and are still popular. The 30-06 cartridge, for instance, has been around since 1906 and the .270 since the 1920s. The .308 was introduced in the early 1950s and the .243 (which is a .308 with a reduced neck size to accommodate a smaller bullet) a few years later. The venerable 6.5x55, which has a devoted following among many stalkers, first appeared as long ago at 1891. These calibres have retained their popularity for such a long time simply because they do their job well, and you can walk into any gunsmith and expect to find them on the shelves. Other calibres come and go, and unless you are a home loader you may have difficulty finding suitable ammunition for your rifle.

Do beware of recoil. I recall a friend turning up to zero a brand new lightweight hunting rifle, unmoderated, in a calibre with a reputation for a punishing kick. Previously he had owned, and shot well with, a .243. To cut a long story short, two boxes of ammunition later he had developed a dreadful flinch and failed to produce anything approaching a reasonable shot grouping on the target. He eventually went back to his old .243. It's true that, today, moderators will reduce recoil considerably with some of the heavier calibres, but it's important not to over-face yourself with too much gun. It's far better to try a variety of calibres before you commit yourself; club range days or stalking friends will be of great help here.

Above all, don't be tempted to go for a large calibre in the expectation that it will kill deer more efficiently. Correct bullet placement is the key, and any legal deer calibre will do the job properly if the bullet is put in the right place. You may have noticed my entirely personal emphasis on two particular calibres, the .243 and .308. That's simply because they have both worked well for me and, if we go back to our arguing group of stalkers, it's fairly clear what the issue is. The truth is that everyone is right. They have each found a calibre that works for them and, over the years, used it successfully, learned its ballistic properties, and as a result developed confidence in it. Choose wisely to begin with and you will do the same.

Travelling Abroad

If you intend to hunt abroad with your rifle, you need to be aware that some countries do not permit private individuals to possess calibres that are used for military purposes. These can include the .308 Winchester (7.62x51mm NATO) or .223 Remington (5.56x45mm NATO), 6.5x55mm Swedish and others which have military counterparts. It's always worth checking with the appropriate embassy when planning your trip.

Rifle Weight Versus Recoil

The weight of a rifle absorbs energy, and thus reduces recoil. It's easy to produce a rifle in the largest calibre and still keep the kick to a minimum; the problem is that it would probably be too heavy to carry all day! The construction of sporting rifles tends, therefore, to be a compromise between overall weight and recoil. One way of further reducing recoil is to use a sound moderator, another is by fitting a muzzle brake.

I don't know how many lions and leopards I've shot. I've shot two elephants, which was enough – never again. It's a melancholy and moving thing to hunt an elephant. It's like shooting an old man. **Wilbur Smith**

WHAT'S IN A NAME?

**THE ORIGINS OF DEER NAMES
AND SOME OF THE LANGUAGE THAT SURROUNDS THEM**

We tend to take their names for granted, but have you ever wondered how the different species of deer came by them, or indeed about the language that has grown up around hunting them? It is a fascinating subject in its own right for, as with all animals, deer take their names from a wide variety of sources. The word 'deer' itself is believed to be derived from the Old English *dor*, which evolved into the Middle English *der*, meaning a swift, wild animal. Plenty of associations have grown up around this word – for example, the city of Derby is said to owe its name to an association with a deer park.

COMMON NAMES

Our native British deer are all named for their colour, most obviously the red deer for the appearance of its summer coat. The others are a little more archaic, though. The name of the roe comes from the Anglo-Saxon *ro*, meaning 'red haired' for its rich, foxy-red summer pelage. Fallow deer may not be truly native to Britain, but they have been here so long that we tend to treat them as such. Their title does not come as you might have thought from fallow or uncultivated ground, but actually from the Old English *fealu*, which refers to a pale brown or yellow colour.

Many deer species simply get their names from the word for deer in their countries of origin – the sika, taken from the Japanese *shika*, is one example. The muntjac takes its name from the word *muntjak* in the Sundanese dialect of Java, either meaning simply a deer, or describing something graceful and bounding. Others, such as the Père David's deer and the Reeves' muntjac found in Britain, are associated with the person who first made the species known to Western science or is credited with bringing the first specimens to Europe. Yet others, such as the Chinese water deer, swamp deer or pampas deer, are named for their preferred habitats. Some more recently identified species, like the Truong Son and Gongshan muntjacs, are named after the national parks in which scientists first discovered them.

DESCRIPTIVE NAMES

Sometimes a name is more descriptive. The barasingha of India comes from the Hindu *bara*, 'twelve', and *singha*, 'horn'. Both the North American wapiti and moose take their names from native American languages – *wapiti* means 'white' (referring to the white rump of the animal) in Shawnee, and moose derives from the Algonquin *mōswa* which translates alternatively as 'the one that strips bark' or 'eater of twigs'. Likewise the caribou, as the reindeer is known in North America, derives its name from *yalipu*, the name given to them by the Micmac Indians of north-eastern Canada and turned into Canadian French. It means 'snow shoveller', a reference to the animal's ability to dig through snow with its specially adapted antlers to reach forage buried beneath. One of the most wonderfully descriptive names for a deer, though, has to be the Chinese for the milu or Père David's deer, *Sen-pou-siang*, which translates loosely as 'none of the four', a reference to this species being reputed to have the antlers of a deer, tail of a donkey, hooves of a cow and neck of a camel!

LATIN NAMES

Latin names can also tell us a lot. The Latin for the roe deer, *capreolus*, means 'little goat', and it is probably for this reason that we refer to a young roe as a kid rather than as a fawn or calf. The word fawn itself has nothing to do with colour; it comes from the Latin *fetus*, originally meaning 'an offspring' rather than the modern day reference to a developing mammal still in the womb. Interestingly, the goat connection persists in the Welsh for fallow, *gafrdanas*, meaning 'goat deer', presumably because a fallow might be compared in size to a large domestic goat. The Chinese water deer, *Hydropotes inermis*, translates as 'unarmed water drinker', reflecting its lack of antlers and preference for wetland habitats. The red deer, *Cervus elaphus*, is unusually a mixture of Latin and Greek; each word translates the same, giving the meaning of 'deer deer'.

THE LANGUAGE OF HUNTING

A rich and varied language has also grown up around the hunting of deer, none less so here in Britain, but with its origins in Europe. It was the Norman invaders who really formalised the status of deer as a quarry reserved for the nobility and strict, often cruel, penalties were applied to those who dared to infringe any of the new laws. The wide vocabulary that surrounded hunting reflected its importance. While the term venison today applies exclusively to deer meat, it originates from the Latin *venari*, meaning 'to hunt'. 'Venerie' or 'venery' was an alternative word for hunting, and quarry was divided through a complicated system into beasts of the chase, beasts of venery and simply vermin; the first two categories were very much the preserve of the aristocratic or 'gentle' hunter, and venison as a term was applied not only to the meat of deer, but also to that of wild boar and other beasts of the chase.

The red and the fallow were the most important deer to the medieval huntsman, probably because they could be relied upon to provide a more exciting pursuit on horseback. The roe, on the other hand, seems to have had a lesser status. The terms stag and hind, and buck and doe, seem to have their origins in Middle English and were most likely specifically used to denote these first two species, but gradually applied to all others as well. Many have largely fallen out of use; unless you live in the West Country you don't often hear a mature red deer referred to as a hart, or a two-year-old as a brocket, but fallow stalkers still commonly use the terms pricket, sore, sorrel, bare buck and great buck to describe bucks at the various stages of their development. There are also regional variations, such as a red stag that has failed to grow antlers being known as a hummel in Scotland, or a nott in the West Country. The red was once known as the fairy deer in the Highlands of Scotland, as it was believed that fairies would milk them on the high mountain-tops.

Royal deer

Under ancient forest law, the red stag was the most important of the beasts of the chase and was classified as a Royal Beast; the second tine of the antler, which we know today as the bay, was known in Norman times as the royal antler. The practice of designating a red stag with twelve points to his antlers as a Royal, or fourteen as an Imperial, is probably a more recent invention of the Victorians, led by Prince Albert, for whom deer stalking took on renewed popularity as a fashionable activity. Confusingly, in the United States, a Royal wapiti is expected to bear a total of fourteen symmetrical points.

What a complex and fascinating subject the naming of deer, and the language of the hunting of them, can be. So, when the actual stalk is over, why not delve into a good book in front of the fire and take the experience to a whole new level?

Get the name right! How often do you hear talk of a red buck, or perhaps a fallow stag? While names may not really seem that important, getting them wrong can imply that the speaker doesn't know what he is talking about. Here is a simple guide:

	Male	Female	Young
Red and Sika	Stag	Hind	Calf
Fallow	Buck	Doe	Calf or Fawn
Roe	Buck	Doe	Kid
Muntjac and CWD	Buck	Doe	Fawn

WHEN DOES A ROE KID

BECOME A YEARLING?

Very often the definition of 'a yearling' can vary according to the person to whom you are speaking. Many observers of roe tend to apply the description primarily to a young buck, born the previous year, carrying its first adult set of antlers. For others, the animal becomes known as a yearling when the buck season opens. By comparison, in horse-racing terms the birthday of all thoroughbreds is arbitrarily set at the first day of January, at which time a foal born at any date during the preceding year is reckoned to be a yearling.

It is difficult to be exact about dates where deer are concerned. Roe birthing usually occurs sometime during April and May, though it sometimes takes place earlier or later. Antler growth and cleaning can also be variable, and as the term yearling applies equally to does as well as to bucks, we cannot base any definition on this either. By the time a roe reaches an age of around thirteen months it will have developed a full set of adult teeth, so perhaps this is a more helpful pointer.

Many deer managers consider the young roe to be a kid whilst it remains 'at heel'. Once it has left its mother in the spring they will then rate it as a yearling. Most biologists, however, refer to an animal as a yearling on its first birthday, so technically we would not be far off setting this date as 1st May. Practically, we can stretch the dates to include culled animals so 1st April seems a sensible compromise.

WHITE DEER

In Britain, only the fallow deer naturally occurs in a white variety. Fallow come in a number of colours, most usually described as common, menil, black and white, although there can be some variations between these main colour phases. The white variety of fallow is quite normal but is not in fact a true albino. Albino deer have pink skin and pink irises to their eyes; white fallow have normal eye pigmentation, although their hooves and noses might be somewhat paler than the other colour varieties.

Black or melanistic fallow are very common, and indeed seem to be the dominant fallow colour variety in some areas. Melanism is caused by an over-production of a chemical called melanin, which causes darker pigmentation in animals. Albinism is caused by a lack of melanin.

White fallow are not so common in the wild, although they are often to be found in deer parks; one famous herd is kept at Houghton Hall in Norfolk. White deer of any kind stand out easily to predators against most backgrounds, and it is for this reason that wild deer managers are split in their attitude towards whether or not to preserve them. On one hand, their presence makes it easier to spot herds containing better camouflaged animals, whilst on the other their especially high visibility can attract poachers.

Occasionally, white animals are seen amongst the other deer species. White red deer are sometimes seen in the wild, and a few exist in park herds. White sika have been regularly observed in recent years in the Purbeck area of Dorset, and white roe are also occasionally seen. Very often, though, these animals are not actually pure white, but simply have paler coats than the norm. Sometimes piebald deer have been recorded, most often roe but occasionally muntjac as well. One famous piebald roe was a buck that lived close to the whisky distillery at Glenfarclas: whilst he was white on one flank and hindquarters, his twin brother was of perfectly normal roe colouration. One can only wonder at what went through visitors' heads on seeing him after touring the distillery and sampling some of its products…

WHITE-TAILED DEER WORLDWIDE

The white-tailed deer, *Odocoileus virginianus*, is native to the Americas, and has a range stretching from southern Canada through most of the United States, Mexico, and Central America, and then into the north-west end of South America. It is generally similar in size to our fallow, although some of the many sub-species may attain only the size of a small roe. The antlers of the buck tend to curve forwards and slightly inwards, giving it a very distinctive appearance. It is evolutionarily related to the European roe: although it does not share the latter species' ability to delay implantation of the fertilised egg after mating, it is similarly a solitary deer that is most often encountered alone or in small family groups.

It is certainly true that there are white-tailed deer, colloquially referred to as whitetail, living free in Europe. In the late 1930s some eleven animals from Minnesota were deliberately released in Finland; by the 1950s these were estimated to have increased to around 300. Today, they have increased to an estimated population of some 55,000 animals. They range across central and southern Finland and have also been recorded as crossing the border into Sweden. They represent by far the most successful European introduction of this species.

Although attempts to acclimatise white-tailed deer in Bulgaria failed, they were more successful in Czechoslovakia where the species was introduced in 1840. Their introduction has never, however, been as successful as it was in Finland, although a small, free-living population remains in the Czech Republic in an area some 50 kilometres to the south of Prague.

Further east, white-tailed deer were introduced to a number of Serbian enclosed localities with varying success in the 1970s and there are also believed to be a few present in Croatia; however, their distribution is extremely limited and numbers are low.

Attempts by the Victorians, who so successfully introduced sika, muntjac and Chinese water deer to our country, to introduce white-tailed deer to England were failures. Some did well initially at Woburn but eventually died out. A more successful attempt in the early 1900s introduced the species to New Zealand, where viable but localised populations still exist today.

A Vindictive Hunter

My packing list for a Continental driven hunt included a high visibility jacket, essential to ensure that neighbouring guns, armed with large calibre rifles and often positioned several hundred metres apart, could easily pick each other out. Luckily I already had one in the car, issued to me in the UK by the police, for humane animal despatch call-outs. Although it had 'HAD' in large letters on the back, it fitted the requirement just nicely.

The shooting party was international and included a couple of Danes. From the outset it was clear that they found something very funny indeed but they insisted on keeping it to themselves until the end of the first day's drives. Eventually they came clean and shared the joke. It was my hi-vis jacket; to the great amusement of everyone present, apparently I was walking around with the Danish word for 'hatred' boldly printed between my shoulder blades.

WHO OWNS WILD DEER?

Wild deer in this country belong to nobody; the law describes them as *ferae naturae* (wild animals) and *rex nullius* (things without an owner). This means that they have no status as property and are free to roam anywhere. As long as they remain wild no person has the right to consider deer as being 'theirs'.

Individuals can, however, hold a right to take deer, whether it is through ownership of the land in question or through the grant of sporting rights. In Scotland this goes further: the Deer (Scotland) Act 1996 allows the Deer Commission for Scotland to kill deer beyond the rights of the owner if it deems that numbers are not being properly controlled.

Deer become property only when they are 'reduced into possession', usually through their legal killing, or if they are found dead on the owner's land for any other reason. So, if a stalker shoots a deer that runs before falling dead on a neighbour's ground, he has no right to cross the boundary and remove the carcase without permission. In the same way, a deer hit by a car is the property of the person owning the place where the deer was killed. The driver has no right to the carcase, nor does he have any claim against anyone for the damage done to his vehicle. However, if a stalker shoots and wounds a deer which subsequently runs onto a public highway and causes an accident, it might be adjudged that he could have foreseen the risk and he could then be held responsible.

Captive deer are different. They are seen as property that can be stolen, provided that proof of ownership can be demonstrated. Even if they escape and are subsequently shot by someone having the sporting rights to the land they are taken on, the original owner has a reasonable demand for the return of the carcase as long as suitable proof of ownership (such as an ear tag) exists. It is worth noting that any exotic species not usually found in this country would fall into such a category; it would be difficult to reason that such an animal (or even a native species bearing a clearly visible sign of ownership) was wild and a charge of criminal damage could easily result from shooting it.

ZOONOSES

CAN DEER PASS ANY DISEASES ON TO HUMANS, AND SHOULD I BE WORRIED?

The simple answer is – yes and no! Although deer can carry some diseases that also affect humans, it is very rare indeed for them to be passed on.

A disease that can pass between vertebrate animals and humans is correctly termed a *zoonosis*. Some that figure prominently in recent world news include Avian influenza (bird flu), Ebola hemorrhagic fever (of primarily African concern, and connected largely with fruit bats and monkeys), and rabies, probably the most feared of the zoonoses in Europe. None of these diseases are especially associated with deer. The main zoonotic disease in this country that can affect deer is bovine tuberculosis, although I have been unable to find any UK record of it ever having been passed between deer and humans. Another major zoonosis associated with deer is anthrax, unrecorded in the UK but present on the Continent, in Africa and in the Americas.

A major observation of zoonoses worth stressing is that close contact between humans and animals is required for them to be transmitted. For example, in the case of bird flu, recorded human cases have all occurred where poultry owners have shared their living areas with the diseased birds, a common practice in some parts of the world. Many Western outbreaks of zoonotic diseases have been traced back to fairs or 'petting zoos', where the public have come into uncontrolled close contact with animals.

So in real terms, you should not be worried as the chances of catching a transferable disease from deer are very low indeed (although stalkers should always take sensible precautions when handling carcases).

There is one disease that all countryside users should be aware of, however, and that is Lyme disease. It is named after Lyme, Connecticut, the town in the USA where it was first identified in the 1970s. The disease affects both deer and humans but is not strictly zoonotic, being passed on by ticks. Although it is not common in the UK, it is wise to keep an eye on any tick bite. Symptoms can take anything between a few days and some weeks to develop, but can include a rash spreading from the site of the tick bite, flu-like symptoms, tiredness, headaches, and joint or muscle pains. If in any doubt a visit to the doctor is highly recommended just to be on the safe side. You can greatly reduce the risk of infection by removing the tick within twenty-four hours of attachment, and taking care not to squeeze it in any way during this process.

Tales from Glen Garron

Touch Not the Cat

Sometimes, knowing too much
can have unwelcome consequences

Willie Cameron was not one to hold a grudge. Even here in Glen Garron, where families had lived and prospered for generations and memories were long, he was known as a fair man who could forgive and forget as well as the next. However, he could not help but be irritated by the newcomer. It didn't matter that the man was English, nor that he had bought the old manse only a year ago and spent a small fortune modernising it in the most ostentatious manner.

Willie had not even been too concerned when the Englishman had taken the sporting lease on a thousand acres of moor and forestry that marched with the estate where he himself was head stalker. Now, though, he was regularly losing some of his better stags whenever they strayed across the boundary, and the forestry was turning into something of a nature reserve for a growing number of hinds and spikers that never seemed to be controlled. It was quickly becoming clear that the man was greedy and unselective in his shooting, and on top of that it seemed he also considered himself an expert on everything.

Nicholas Highworth ('Call me Nick, my dear fellow, no need to be formal') had moved to the Highlands from Surrey, where he had made a great deal of money selling used cars before deciding to retire early to indulge his passions for stalking and fishing. He had brought with him a wife who complained incessantly about the primitive conditions she was now forced to endure after the delights of Godalming. On the positive side, he also had an attractive, cheerful daughter called Amanda who had taken to village life like a duck to water and now worked behind the bar of the local pub. The younger local lads, Willie's boy Archie included, were already competing for her attention like stags on the high tops in October.

The problem with Nick was that he knew too much. Nothing gave him more pleasure than holding court nightly in the saloon bar of the Kelpie Inn on the complexities of stalking, ballistics, fly patterns – you name it, he knew about it all. He was adept at taking over a conversation, overruling everyone else and always having the last word.

This evening was no exception. Willie and a few friends from the neighbouring estates had been enjoying a quiet chat about the prospects for the coming grouse-breeding season when a crunch of gravel outside announced Nick's arrival in his gleaming new silver Land Rover, complete with heated seats, winch and snorkel. Joining them uninvited, Nick had then proceeded to hold forth to his unwilling audience of gamekeepers and stalkers on the benefits of medicated grouse grit and why the .270 Winchester was by far the best calibre for Highland stalking. Willie recognised a great deal of material from last week's *Shooting Times*, repeated almost verbatim.

As Nick left the table to refresh his pint, Willie reflected that not once in the last twelve months had he offered to buy one for anyone in the group he was drinking with. That, for Willie, was the last straw. The new man clearly gave no thought to his neighbours, had far too inflated a view of himself and badly needed to be brought down to earth; the question was, how? Willie's eyes drifted to a picture behind the bar, and slowly a smile creased his face. He leaned across the table and told his friends what he had in mind.

The grainy, black-and-white press cutting behind the bar showed a beaming crofter alongside a cage containing a rather scruffy and dejected looking mountain lion. The big cat had escaped from a wildlife park far to the south and had turned up in Glen Garron, thin and starving, a fortnight later when the crofter had trapped it in his barn. Willie, who had been on hand at the time, got the impression that the animal had been more than happy to surrender itself to the comforts of captivity when the park staff had arrived to reclaim it, and always thought that the blaring headlines proclaiming 'Beast in Custody – Glen Safe!' were a bit strong. Now he called Archie over and gave him strict instructions for when he was next chatting to the fair Amanda.

The fly was cast, although it took a good week for it to be taken; but Willie eventually found himself being questioned about the cat. 'Aye,' he told the transfixed Nick as they examined the press cutting over a pint at the Kelpie, 'the park swore that they'd nae lost but the one, but there's been rare sounds in the night, aye, and sheep going missing. I'll no credit it, mind, but there are those who give talk of dark beasties crossing the roads at night. More fool them, I say.'

Nick, on the other hand, was not so dismissive. 'Don't count on it, old fellow. There are plenty of stories of big cats down south. They say that a keeper down in Essex has a black panther in his freezer – apparently he shot it when doing his rounds one morning but can't make it public in case he loses his Firearms Certificate. Dangerous things, too – apparently when they attack they'll try and open you up with their back claws.' With this he was away on another flight of knowledge, and it took Willie a good half-hour to escape Nick's summary of big cat evidence in the UK. Before he left, though, he made sure to mention a big roe buck he'd seen regularly on the march between Glen Garron and Nick's forestry block. 'Thanks, old fellow. I'll have a look there tomorrow night.'

The following morning, Archie found Willie in his workshop, hammering six-inch nails though a short piece of timber. When his father told him what he was about, the son fell about laughing. 'When you've finished blathering, boy,' he was told, 'give old McDaid a call up at the farm and see if he's got any fallen stock. And see if your friend Angus has still got that wee toy o' his.'

It was getting dark when an agitated Nick burst into the Kelpie Inn. 'Proof!' he announced to a packed house. 'I've got proof of your beast!' At his insistence a small convoy of vehicles made their way up to the forestry block, where, by lamp-light, Nick excitedly pointed out some long scratch marks four feet up the trunk of a pine. 'And that's not all!' he continued. 'Look!' He directed the lamp beam towards the top of the tree. Wedged firmly in a high fork among the branches was the eviscerated carcase of a well-grown lamb.

'Weel, there's nothing else for it,' Willie announced. 'We'll have to find whatever did this. It'll be awfy dangerous, but we canna leave it roaming oot there.'

He got no further. Out of the darkness came a series of guttural grunts, terrifyingly close. The party retreated quickly to the nearest Land Rover. Rather shaky lamp beams scanned the surrounding silent forest.

'I'll get it, Da!' cried Archie, and before anyone could stop him had retrieved his shotgun and a torch from his pickup and advanced into the gloom in the direction of the noise. 'Come awa', ye glaikit child', Willie called after him anxiously. For the next few minutes all that could be seen was a torch beam flickering through the trees. Suddenly two gunshots sounded in quick succession, followed by a feral screech and then the scream of a human in mortal pain, and the light went out.

For a moment there was a shocked silence in the Land Rover. Willie flicked on the headlights to illuminate a figure staggering back towards them clutching his stomach. Archie's face was a mask of blood, and his Army surplus combat jacket was ripped and shredded. He collapsed to the ground and, to Nick's horror, a long, slippery tube of something unspeakable escaped from the ruins of his coat.

For a moment there was a shocked silence, then Willie took charge. 'You!' he snapped, pointing at Nick. 'Get awa' to the village and wake the doctor. We'll look after puir Archie.'

Nick needed no further prompting. White-faced and anxious to be away from the dreadful scene, he leapt into his shiny new Land Rover and sped off, wheels spinning, down the rough track. The sound of his engine faded into the distance.

'Brawly done, son!' exclaimed Willie.

Archie's eyes opened and a grin split his bloody face. 'I hope you warned the doc,' he replied. He looked around the assembled faces. 'I could do wi' a change – that sheep gralloch was getting fair manky.' He raised his voice. 'Come on out now, Angus, and fetch the tape recorder. By the way, did anyone think to bring the malt with them?'

What none of the laughing group noticed as they made their way back towards the vehicles was a single imprint in the soft mud of the track, a rounded pad mark the size of a small plate which had been made by no shoe or hoof. In the darkness a pair of yellow eyes briefly considered the lamb carcase and decided, reluctantly, that it was better to be elsewhere.

SHORT
STORIES

April Muntjac

A spring stalk for Hampshire muntjac

There are perhaps three basic ways to get to grips with muntjac – go to them, ambush them, or persuade them to come to you. The first involves active stalking, the second a great deal of patience and the third a degree of enticement. Sometimes I like to combine all three. Whilst I know that sitting and waiting in a high seat or simply at a suitable vantage point is most likely to yield results, I do enjoy moving quietly through the woods with constantly changing scenery and the anticipation of what awaits me round the next corner.

Muntjac can move at any time of day when the ground is undisturbed. On one particular sunny mid-April afternoon, I had decided to combine an afternoon stalk with a bit of calling and a sit in one of my doe boxes. Driving onto the patch I picked up the unmistakable call of what was, for me, the first cuckoo of the year. Much of the woodland understorey was still bare for the time of year although wild primroses festooned the grassy banks alongside the track. Elsewhere, the dog's mercury was starting to come through strongly, dotted with the delicate yellow flowers of celandine that close at night and are so appropriately often known as 'spring messenger'. Clumps of daffodils (much too large to be wild ones, so what were they doing so far from human habitation?) decorated the roadside in garish clumps. Yellow certainly seems to be the spring colour in this corner of the world.

As I drove down the track to the main wood, a brief burst of excitement was provided by a fox mousing, in broad daylight, in an adjacent long-grass field. This might have been an opportunity to do the local keeper a favour, but we'll have to draw a discreet veil over events. Rest assured that I caught up with him next time we met.

Parking up in a well-shaded corner, I let Mole out for a quick run. There may be some springers out there who walk quietly at heel without any need for constant reining in, but Mole certainly isn't one of them. Instead, she stays in the car when I'm stalking, my insurance policy in case there is a need for a follow-up on a shot deer. Thankfully this does not happen often, but she has saved me more than one carcase when the animal has run a short distance in thick cover before dropping dead. It's surprising how easy it is to walk past an animal as large as even a fallow lying in a slight dip without noticing it.

Leaving the car, I made my way up the rough track. It's not difficult to move quietly; the trick is to do everything slowly, be aware of where you are putting your feet, and place them down on their outside edges before rolling them inwards. Use your binoculars frequently. You'll be amazed at the extra detail you pick up that the naked eye misses. Never lose track of the fact that your quarry, whether a big fallow or a diminutive muntjac, is looking on a lower plane than you. It often pays to crouch down from time to time and look under cover at the deer's level.

On this occasion, the trunk of a broad oak overlooking a broken area of rough scrub offered a background for me to try a spot of calling. With the rifle set up on the sticks ready for instant use, I tried a few short squeaks on the Buttolo call. After a few minutes and no movement, I made a few more. Out of the corner of my eye I saw movement and slowly turned my head to see the animal: a muntjac doe approaching cautiously down a narrow track about forty yards away. Edging the rifle around to cover it, I waited for it to move forward of a small fallen branch obscuring the shot. Frustratingly, the doe turned off the track into thicker cover and was lost to sight. There was nothing to do but wait. After a few more minutes I tried another series of squeaks with no result. Assuming that the doe had worked out what I was and departed unseen, I decided to move on.

Almost immediately I disturbed another animal, which must also have come in to the call. All I saw was a rump departing from behind a pile of brash, the tail held vertically. When a muntjac holds its tail like that it will not stop until it is in deep cover, although an unsure animal, with tail held horizontally, will often pause to a squeak from the Buttolo or a quietly spoken 'oi'. Not far off in the same direction a fawn, presumably belonging to the departed animal, watched me quizzically for a few moments before making off as well. Still heavily spotted with infant pelage, it was clearly only six or seven weeks old. (Muntjac lose their spots at about two months old, coincidentally the age at which they are weaned.)

Another attempt at calling further on proved to be equally frustrating. This time two muntjac, a small buck and a doe, crossed in front between some scattered clumps of rhododendron on higher ground with a restricted backstop for the bullet where a shot would have been foolhardy. Muntjac can respond to a call in many ways. Sometimes they will come cautiously and try to identify the source of the noise, and very often you will believe that there has been no response as they approach in cover, see what you are, and leave just as unobtrusively. At other times they will rush in without hesitation. Be careful with these, as the animal may well be a nursing mother responding to what she thinks are alarm calls from her fawn. In this particular instance, it was the 'I just happen to be passing this way' reaction.

An hour or so sitting in a doe box produced nothing apart from a mature roe buck. In prime condition and with newly cleaned antlers, white and still showing tatters of velvet, he wasn't on the cull plan so I watched him browse on the emerging vegetation for a few minutes before he moved away with no sign of concern.

Time was getting on and I decided to stalk back towards the car. Once again, a small muntjac buck and a larger doe crossed the path, quite possibly the two seen earlier, and once again with a frustrating lack of backstop. Below them, I knew, was a shallow bank and it was quite possible that they might still be in view at the bottom of it. As they passed out of view I moved quickly but cautiously forward. At the bottom of the bank the buck was looking up towards me through the branches of a low tree. It wasn't going to stand there for long. No time for finesse: I crouched down and sought a clear path for the bullet between two branches. As the cross hairs floated onto the chest of the buck a gentle squeeze on the trigger dropped it instantly.

By the time the gralloch was completed, the light had almost gone and it was time to return to the car and make my way home. I had something to show for my efforts, and had enjoyed the added bonus of being out in woods reawakening after a long and dismal winter. Back at the house, there was another treat – with the carcase safely hung in the chiller, a very appropriate supper of homemade muntjac burgers awaited. It was a timely reminder that I'd let freezer stocks fall low – with summer on the way, it was definitely time to make some more!

Muntjac Burgers

- Simply mix finely minced muntjac (or any other) venison with minced belly pork at a ratio of about 4:1, along with a sprinkling of dried mixed herbs of your choice (basil, thyme, oregano or a general mix all work well) and a little seasoning of salt and pepper to taste.
- Form into patties weighing about 4oz each. Using a simple hamburger press helps to ensure that they hold together better when cooking.
- Grill, barbecue or pan-fry them for a few minutes on each side (no extra oil should be necessary if you use a non-stick pan) until the centre of the burger loses its pinkness.
- The burgers freeze very well and are always welcome as a quick and delicious simple supper at any time of year, or for *al fresco* meals when the weather warms up.

Berkeley Square

**Sometimes you can have a memorable evening's stalking
without firing a shot…**

On my little piece of Hampshire stalking ground there is a small grass
meadow, about the size of a football pitch, tucked away in the middle of
some badly overgrown and unmanaged woodland. To one side of it, hidden
by a light screen of blackthorn, lies a small stream, little more than a brook
really, that flows along sleepily enough but supports a myriad of water life.
Mandarin ducks have taken to nesting in the trunks of trees that border it,
and occasionally you can see kingfishers darting like miniature bejewelled
meteors along its length. There are freshwater mussels in its depths; once I
found a number of shells on the bank under a bridge bearing the characteristic
chewed edges made by an otter. Try as I might, I've never seen the animal that
enjoyed them, despite setting up trail cameras which have caught everything
else, including such unwelcome visitors as domestic cats and, on one occasion,
three teenage boys who had no business being there smoking and drinking
canned lager.

The local shoot beats the surrounding woods occasionally, and the
keeper maintains a grain feeder made out of an old oil drum at one end
of the meadow. It was he, in fact, who first brought the area to my closer
attention, complaining that the grain seemed to be mostly feeding 'my' deer.
Close inspection showed up the slots of any number of fallow, which had
trampled a muddy circle around the feeder. Once again the trail cameras
were brought into action, proving that the area was being heavily used not
just by fallow, but also by roe, muntjac, at least three different foxes, and
badgers which came from who knows where, the nearest known sett being
well over a mile away. Reason enough, I thought, to erect a high seat and
hopefully account for a few deer, especially the marauding fallow, to keep
the keeper happy.

There being no suitable tree in a useful place to support a lean-to
seat, it was a question of putting up a free-stander, a sturdy affair based on

continental boar shooting stands and with bricks under the feet to add a few years to its life in the perpetually damp environment. With an approach path cut in through the willows behind it, I was highly confident that a few fallow would soon be called to account.

My expectations were quickly dashed. In the three years since the seat was erected I have yet to see, let alone shoot, a fallow from it, and it has become clear that their visits to the feeder must be almost entirely nocturnal. However, and what a happy accident this was, the location has turned out to be one of my muntjac 'bankers'. I have since taken any number from it, and it is the one place that I can go with a very high expectation of a shot or two. The meadow also seems to draw in foxes; on one occasion I climbed into the seat to find a large dog cub fast asleep on the wood edge not twenty yards away. It, like so many others, was not given the chance to leave and the shoot is certainly happy with my efforts. With an occasional roe also added to the tally, it's not surprising that the place has become one of my favourites for a sit out, and I have to force myself not to over-use it.

The clearing, which I had come to think of as the muntjac meadow, flooded badly during this particular winter and the deer moved elsewhere, but as May approached it dried out and became lush and green once again. It was not, however, until well into the month that I got the chance to visit it, so it was with high expectations that I settled into the seat with a couple of hours of daylight remaining and loaded the rifle. Muntjac, yearling roe bucks and fox were most definitely on the menu, and who knew, a fallow pricket might even decide to step into the open and offer a chance.

The evening was warm enough to persuade me to discard my light coat, and as I settled down to watch a cuckoo called somewhere close by. Half a dozen rabbits, undisturbed by my approach, divided their time between grazing and doing what rabbits do so famously and so frequently. Their courtship chases, involving high twisting leaps into the air, always amuse me and it was clearly not going to be a boring evening whatever else showed up. Half a dozen pheasants, dominated by one pugnacious cock, fed round the oil drum, and were joined by a couple of squirrels. Not for the first time I half wished for the moderated .22 sitting in the cabinet at home.

Something larger, coloured a rich chestnut, moved behind a low bush on the far side of the clearing. I reached involuntarily for the rifle, to relax again as a big roe doe made her way cautiously towards the pheasant feeder. Sides bulging like a barrel, she was obviously not far off birthing and clearly on her own. Pausing only to take a few mouthfuls of grain from the feeder through the light wire screen erected in an ineffectual attempt to exclude deer, she moved unhurriedly across the clearing and disappeared into the blackthorn.

Only a few minutes passed before another roe doe, this time a yearling, appeared from the same place and settled to pluck out some morsels of new plant growth from amongst the grass. She grazed her way gradually towards me, obviously relaxed and unsuspecting of my presence, eventually couching to cud in the evening sun on the wood's edge. She moved on at some point but I didn't notice her go.

About twenty minutes of shooting light remained when I became aware of a small bird starting to sing from only a dozen yards or so away, in the willows behind me. For a moment I failed to identify it, and then suddenly recognised the incredible variety of notes, dipping effortlessly from high to low, full of whistles, chirps and liquid trills as the invisible bird proclaimed its presence to a potential mate, filling the meadow with a powerful and melodious message to the world in a rich medley of sound.

It had been many years since I had last heard a nightingale in full flow, and I'd forgotten the sheer, entrancing virtuosity of these otherwise drab and secretive little birds. If a muntjac or roe buck had appeared just then I don't think that I'd have been prepared to shatter the moment with a shot. Darkness finally came, and the nightingale sang on into the gloom as I continued to sit there, enthralled, by his whistling, churring and gurgling into the night. It was pitch black when I finally forced myself down from the seat and left him, still singing his heart out, to make my way back to the car.

From that moment on the muntjac meadow became, to my mind though never named so on any map, Berkeley Square. It serves to remind me that sometimes you can still have a supremely memorable and fulfilling stalking experience without ever once lifting the rifle.

Estonian Elk

In Estonia on the Baltic coast, in the hope of shooting a first elk

Deep in the Estonian forest the weak afternoon sun was starting to fade. After two driven hunting days and two evening sit outs, I had yet to see a live elk and had only once made out the vague shapes of wild boar in the gloom the night before, so had reluctantly come to the conclusion that this was likely to be a blank week. Happily half of the party had enjoyed success, with a total of five elk, a boar and a raccoon dog between the twelve of us, but otherwise chances had been very thin on the ground and the rest of us had not fired a shot. It looked as though the ridiculously optimistic sixty rounds of ammunition that I'd brought, less the half dozen I'd expended on the national hunter's shooting test, would all be going home with me.

The two days of driving the forest with Swedish elkhounds for elk and boar had been largely unproductive, although I had enjoyed the unforgettable sight of a cock capercaillie landing clumsily in a tree above my head before flying off again. The first evening in a shooting box had produced nothing, but waiting in the stygian gloom below the box to be picked up by a guide it had occurred to me that, unlike home, the woods contained creatures such as bear, boar and wolves. At the end of the second evening I'd elected, rather wimpishly, to wait in the box until the headlights of the pickup were visible.

So now it was the last evening and my final chance of a shot. Roland, our guide from the local hunting association, dropped me off at the base of the tower with about two hours of shooting light remaining. 'Keep the windows closed,' were his parting words, 'the elk smells very well!' The tower loomed above me. Estonian hunting stands are luxurious compared with British standards, but then they need to be if you are waiting all night in sub-zero temperatures for the chance of a boar by moonlight. Tonight's tower was the tallest yet, a massive construction based on concrete and iron legs, on top of which balanced a box you could have accommodated a small family in. As Roland drove off, I started to climb.

The first thing that struck me when I entered the box was the buzzing. Thousands of flies, evidently seeking warmth as autumn showed signs of giving way to winter, had taken up residence. My arrival had disturbed them and they were everywhere: covering the windows and the walls of the box, coating the old car seat welded to a frame provided for the shooter's comfort, and settling briefly on me. I badly wanted to open the shooting windows but heeded Roland's words instead.

The windows themselves could have done with a good clean, but peering through them I could just about make out a large clearing, covering about a hundred and fifty metres in each direction. Half of it had been planted with a root crop, presumably to attract game, and in the centre was the usual bait point of a salt block on top of a six-foot pole adjacent to a pile of grain, which two jays, unconcerned by my arrival, were thoroughly enjoying. Thick forest surrounded the clearing.

With the .308 loaded, I double-checked that the safety was on and placed it in the rifle rack provided in one corner of the box. After briefly considering the car seat with its coating of flies and other unidentified debris, I decided that it wouldn't be too much of a hardship to stand for a couple of hours and moved the seat carefully to one side. I checked the opening mechanisms of the shooting windows – the two side ones tilted upwards and outwards, while the centre one opened inwards. Beyond testing the wooden fastenings I didn't dare to open them any further, but as far as I could tell they would be silent.

I leant against one of the wooden side walls and settled down to wait, occasionally scanning the clearing with my binoculars. The jays tired of the grain heap and departed. Nothing else moved.

An hour and a half later the clearing was still deserted. It was as if I was the only living creature in the vicinity, apart from the flies which had mercifully settled down again. I checked my watch – perhaps another half an hour of shooting light was left – and wondered if anything was going to make an appearance. A nagging feeling that this was going to turn out to be another blank started to grow on me.

Time passed, and a movement at the far side of the root crop away to the right caught my eye. The binoculars revealed a raccoon dog, a strange mixture of fox, badger and of course raccoon, slowly pottering down the edge of the roots towards me. These invasive introductions from the Far East are now well-established in Eastern Europe and were most definitely on the quarry list, so I slowly picked up my rifle and moved to lift the shooting window. Something stopped me, though. I hadn't come all this way for a raccoon dog, so I put down the rifle as it passed to one side of the tower and disappeared into the undergrowth.

Minutes passed and the light was clearly not going to last much longer. As I began to regret passing up the chance of a shot, a presence suddenly announced itself on the far side of the clearing: what initially appeared to be a big black bus stepped out into the open. Even at well over a hundred yards the bull elk looked enormous. Although just a relative youngster with simple spike antlers, to someone more used to muntjac, roe and fallow it was still a leviathan. As I held the binoculars my hands started to shake slightly – not buck fever, please, not now!

Slowly, very slowly, I began to raise the front shooting window and just as carefully slid the rifle barrel out. The elk remained where it was, broadside on and head down in the roots. Once the front end of the scope was clear of the frame I mounted the rifle and placed the red dot of the sight onto the beast's shoulder. Time stood still: and, as usual, the rifle seemed to go off on its own.

Sound moderators are not permitted in Estonia and in the excitement of the moment I'd forgotten to put on the ear defenders that I'd carried against just such an opportunity. The crash of the rifle in the small confines of the box was deafening, and the muzzle flash in the fast-fading light briefly blinded me to the strike. All I was aware of were the white hind legs of my target disappearing back into the trees, and swarms of disturbed flies buzzing angrily to accompany the ringing in my ears.

I stayed where I was and watched, the tension of the moment releasing itself in a brief attack of the shakes. Minutes later Roland, alerted by the shot, appeared below the tower and we walked over to where the elk had been standing. To my great relief the huge animal had only made a few steps before collapsing and lay, dead, at the edge of the forest. Roland's smile was almost as wide as mine as he shook my hand before finding a juniper bush and breaking off two sprigs, one for my hat and one as the 'last bite' for my first, but hopefully not my last, elk.

As I watched Roland expertly gralloch the animal in the headlights of the pickup, an industrial undertaking in its own right, I could not have been happier. I didn't even mind paying the inevitable drinks bill that evening.

Elk Facts

- The European elk *Alces alces* is the same animal as the North American moose. Confusingly, what the Americans call an elk is a different species of deer entirely, closely related to our native red and otherwise known as a wapiti.
- An average bull elk might weigh up to 500kg and stand as high as 2 metres at the shoulder. His unique upturned and palmated antlers can measure 1.5 metres from tip to tip.
- Alaskan animals are considered to be the biggest. The largest ever recorded was shot by the Yukon River in 1897. It weighed 820kg and measured 2.33 metres, or 7 feet 4 inches, at the shoulder.
- The elk rut takes place in September and October. Eight months later the cow gives birth to one or two calves, which will stay with their mother for the next year.
- Elk have a varied diet, which includes aquatic plants. They are excellent swimmers and are the only deer capable of feeding underwater.
- The world population of elk is healthy and increasing. There may be as many as one million in Canada alone, and Newfoundland's estimated population of about 150,000 has descended from just four animals introduced to the island in 1904.

Fallow Follow-Up

'Come on over', said Dave's voice on the telephone. 'I'm getting a party together to fill some seats.' The fallow doe season had just opened and Dave was keen to make a quick start to the cull, so the more high seats he could have occupied that night, the better. Unsure of what the evening would entail, I decided to leave the dog at home as it was an unusually sunny early November evening and I didn't want to risk leaving her in the car. As my .308 was still awaiting a check zero after fitting a new scope, I had to take the .243 instead. Both decisions, as it turned out, were to have a bearing on later events.

After a quick mug of tea and a chat, Dave loaded fellow guest Jaimie onto the back of his quad bike and set off to place him in his high seat for the evening. Soon he was back for me and we were bumping over the rough tracks to my position. The seat was a solid metal construction, easily big enough to accommodate two people in comfort and fixed solidly to a large oak. The previous occupant had even thoughtfully turned the seat over so that I had a dry plank to sit on. The sheet of foam that I carry in my waist bag for such occasions added to my comfort and helped to ensure that I would be able to avoid fidgeting or moving around too much for the coming couple of hours. Taking care that my muzzle was pointed safely towards the ground below, I chambered a round, checked that the safety catch was on, and settled down to wait.

The wind was starting to get up and the trees around me were being blown about quite violently. I had not been sitting for more than a few minutes when a loud report echoed through the woods, followed after a few seconds by another one. As I wondered what had transpired, the mobile phone in my pocket vibrated silently. I slowly fished it out to check the message, which was from Jaimie: it simply said 'Two fallow'. Later he told me that the animals had appeared some fifty yards away, and that when he shot the doe the follower, a buck calf, had hesitated, no doubt uncertain over the source of the moderated shot, allowing him the opportunity to take that as well.

What an excellent start to the evening. Despite the strong winds, it was relatively sheltered and warm where I was sitting and the tree supporting my seat had been well selected to be stable and secure. Half a dozen cock pheasants fed among the scattered stray on the ride in front of me and I couldn't suppress a smile as a young muntjac, only a few months old, seemed to be deliberately taunting one of them by skipping at it and repeatedly forcing the pheasant to give way. There was no sign of the mother and I had no difficulty in deciding to leave the youngster in peace. It eventually disappeared into some dense brambles at the side of the ride.

The light was just starting to show signs of fading when two more shots, one from Jaimie's direction and another, louder – which I correctly assumed to be Dave – announced two more fallow does in the bag. By this point I had seen no sign of any deer, and was just beginning to give up hope when I caught movement among the trees out of the corner of my eye. Careful examination through the binoculars enabled me to make out a fallow buck, a sorrel, steadily making its way towards me. There was no clear view through the undergrowth so I had to wait for it to reach a clear patch where I would have a fair chance of a shot. The fallow reached the clearing and just kept on walking. By now the rifle was in the shoulder with safety catch off but the opportunity was about to disappear.

There was only one thing for it; I pursed my lips and made a sharp squeak. Instantly the buck stopped, tensed, raised its head and looked in my direction. It was clearly about to run, but it was the work of an instant to float the cross hairs onto its chest and squeeze the trigger. The report of the rifle covered any sound of bullet strike, but the buck jumped, all feet off the ground, before crashing off into the undergrowth. I quickly chambered another round and watched, but saw no further movement.

The light was now beginning to disappear fast. I unloaded, climbed down and made my way carefully to where the buck had been standing when it was hit and looked in vain for any signs of bullet strike. This didn't worry me too much. I was confident of a killing shot, and knew that the little 100 grain .243 bullet seldom produces a sizeable exit wound on a larger deer, if indeed it exits at all. However, there was no time left before night fell completely and the animal had to be found without delay.

My bag yielded a head torch and the search was on. Normally at this point I would have fetched the dog, who would have taken me to the buck in no time, but of course she was at home. Sweeping backwards and forwards across the buck's line of flight yielded no signs of blood: had I actually hit it? I discounted the doubts and started to walk in a grid, pacing out fifty yards and turning for a few more before heading back towards the start point, marked with a tiny strobe light which I carry to clip onto the dog's collar for night work. By now it was pitch black and my small torch only produced limited light. The woodland was mainly coppice, so I felt confident that I was covering it efficiently, but several times I lost my bearings and had to start again. Of the buck, however, there was no sign.

Fortunately at this point the other shot animals had been recovered, and approaching headlights announced the arrival of my fellow stalkers. This time we formed an extended line, all with torches, and walked forward to find my sorrel lying dead to a heart shot only twenty yards or so from where I had shot it. I must have passed it several times during my solo search but failed to spot it. It's surprising how easy it is to miss an animal even as big as a fallow, especially if it's lying with its back to you and not exposing the lighter belly hair.

Back at the larder, with five carcases for the evening's work, we all shared similar stories of 'lost' animals, and expressed relief that the buck had been recovered quickly rather than having to be left out overnight. At the same time I made a personal resolution not to leave the dog behind next time.

Lessons from the Evening

- A trained dog saves a lot of searching.
- As a general rule, smaller, faster calibres don't deliver as much terminal energy for 'knock down' as larger, slower ones.
- If the animal is on the alert when shot, don't be surprised if it runs on a short way before collapsing, even if well hit.
- Don't always expect to find obvious signs of a strike and a strong blood trail.
- Always assume a hit, even when there are no immediate signs of a strike.
- If you have to search without a dog, mark your starting point well so that you can return to it if necessary, and be methodical. A large deer can often be hard to spot, even when lying on fairly clear ground.

The First

Simon and I followed the scrubby belt down, with the warm wind in our faces. Ahead of us, rabbits and the odd pheasant, suddenly aware of our cautious progress, moved hastily into cover but nothing larger showed. Somewhere up ahead I was sure there was a buck. Simon had spotted it briefly from the top of the hill through the trees before it had moved out of vision. Worth a go, we agreed, if only to have a look and see how good it was. I didn't hold out much hope of a cull as I thought I knew which animal it would be – a mature six-pointer that I intended to leave this year. Still, always worth a look…

It had already been an eventful May morning. Simon, having just acquired and zeroed his new rifle, had called the night before to say that he was free and could we go out? This was his first armed outing and he was so keen that I couldn't refuse.

At the agreed time next morning Simon climbed into my ancient Land Rover and we set off, hopefully not waking too many sleeping neighbours in the process. With the wind in the south-west, an approach from the far side of the area was called for. The Land Rover struggled manfully up the hill on the southerly main road at a steady forty mph. A sad sight confronted us as we reached the top. In the centre of the road lay a young roe doe kicking fitfully – the result of a hit-and-run. Next to her stood another, which made off as we approached. There were no other cars in sight.

I stopped, instructed Simon to keep an eye open for traffic, and quickly put the animal out of its misery before loading it into the back of the Land Rover. Not the best way to start a novice's first outing but lessons could be learnt nonetheless. Safely out of public view on the stalking area, Simon completed his first gralloch, with no need to worry about bodging it – the doe was in such a mess I doubted that there would even be much dog meat to salvage. Later, I rang the police to check that no one had reported the accident and asked them to inform the council, as legal owners of the carcase. They confirmed that the latter would not have wanted it anyway. Still, better safe than sorry.

Time was getting on and we only had an hour before we were due to be off the ground. It was then, as we glassed the ground from the top of the hill, that Simon spotted a roe moving some half a mile away the other side of a shelter belt of young trees and scrub. He was sure it was a buck but it had fed back behind the belt before I could get my binoculars onto it. I had certainly seen one in that area several times already that month, a big, mature fellow carrying a potential medal head. Definitely not for the cull but certainly worth a closer look, if only for interest. The wind was perfect for the more direct approach so off we went.

We moved in slowly. Suddenly, only fifty yards ahead, what looked like a four-point yearling jumped out of the shelter belt, stood briefly, then jumped in again. I froze. Simon, betraying his military training, opted for the dash to cover. The buck didn't seem to notice us – stroke of luck number one. It was out of sight again but seemed to be coming our way slowly. We moved back gently to a gap in the belt that offered clear shooting to both sides and thick blackthorn in front and waited. The animal had to come either side of the blackthorn, I reasoned, as I whispered for Simon to stand by.

I was wrong. The buck came straight through the middle of the blackthorn and froze as it saw our motionless, kneeling shapes. It immediately backed off the way it had come. Simon's shoulders slumped in an expression of missed opportunity. 'Wait', I whispered. 'He'll be back.'

Stroke of luck number two – he didn't let me down. Uncertain of what the strange shapes were, curiosity overcame common sense. I have no doubt that if this had been an older animal we would not have seen him for dust. Desperate to get our scent and find out what we were, which meant getting behind us, the buck broke cover and skirted us at about thirty yards range. Stiff-legged and neck craning, he was obviously tense and ready to flee instantly but just couldn't decide whether or not we were dangerous. Several times he tried to get around us but lost his nerve and doubled back, only to try again and again, never still for more than a second. Eventually a quiet squeak through pursed lips stopped him broadside with the grassy hillside behind him, which offered the opportunity that we had been waiting for. Simon did not waste it. Plenty of practice on the paper buck target had taught him exactly where to place the shot and the buck fell instantly – stroke of luck number three, considering the adrenaline that must have been in his system.

After a quiet reminder from me to reload, we watched the buck kick once and then lie still. We approached cautiously and found that he had expired on the spot. Now was the time for congratulations and to let the tension of the last few minutes subside. Simon was man enough to admit that he was shaking like a leaf, and I was pleased to note the familiar expression of regret mixed with pleasure at the achievement as we examined the carcase.

The little 87 grain bullet from Simon's .243 was well placed but had deflected off a rib and turned ninety degrees. We felt it resting between skin and haunch and recovered it later, perfectly mushroomed, when skinning out. The result, of course, was two messy grallochs in one morning – bad luck for a first outing but Simon seemed to take it all in his stride. An examination of the teeth showed that the animal was not a yearling as I had thought but a poor two-year-old – just the sort of cull animal for which we had been looking.

The trophy now has pride of place on Simon's wall – its light four points are not the most impressive head but remain a lasting reminder of an eventful morning and his first roebuck.

High Times

Some high-seat experiences – good and bad

Some time ago I was sitting in a high seat somewhere in Norfolk waiting for a muntjac or fallow to show. The seat was a wonderfully solid, free-standing affair built from treated wood, with a proper floor and skirted with camouflage netting. It placed me a good twelve feet above the ground, with clear views out to about a hundred and fifty yards on either side, covering a well-maintained feed ride with grain hoppers sited every fifty yards or so. The evening took a slightly surreal turn as I realised that it was not pheasants coming to the feeders, but duck – dozens of mallard flighting in to take advantage of the grain. As I watched, one of the biggest rats I have ever seen took over one of the feed hoppers, seeing off two other rats and a rabbit twice its size before even facing down a mallard drake. A heavy thump startled me into turning round, to find myself face-to-face with a very large peahen perched clumsily on the shooting rail. I'm not sure which of us was the more alarmed, but she launched off quickly and awkwardly, brushing my face with a wing tip and leaving me, heart thumping, to await whatever other surprises the evening might bring.

All this started me thinking about some of the other high seats that I have experienced over the years. Some have slid out of my memory, but others, for a variety of reasons, have etched themselves indelibly on it. Perched still and quiet at branch level certainly brings any number of close encounters with wildlife – I've had a wood pigeon settle briefly on the rifle barrel, a kingfisher on the shooting rail a few feet from my face, and any number of angry squirrels chittering at the unidentified object invading their territory. One barn owl took up residence in a German-style box seat on my patch – always delightful to see, but a distinct shock to a visiting stalker who hadn't been warned to leave space for it to exit past his shoulder when climbing in through the trap-door base. Once, hunting moose in Quebec, I was joined in my ground hide at the edge of a swamp by a porcupine – but that's another story entirely!

You'll often hear people say that deer don't look up. That's not entirely true, but I've certainly found that humans are not always aware of what is going on above head height. Perhaps our more evolved senses have been dulled to the threat of predators approaching from above? In my experience, the Great British Public, thinking themselves unobserved, can get up to all kinds of things. Reports persist of the naked Surrey jogger who has been spotted by several people over the past few years, and occasionally a discreet cough can be necessary to warn people that somebody is watching their antics from on high…

Years ago I was sitting overlooking a Hampshire wood edge one warm summer's evening, waiting for a roe buck to appear. After I had been there only a short while, a rather large lady, accompanied by an even larger labrador, suddenly appeared from the woodline to my right and made her way out across the meadow in front of me. As I was a guest and not really sure who she was or whether she had a right to be there, I decided to sit tight and let her make her way over the hill. After all, it was at least an hour until last light and the area would quickly settle down again after the two of them had gone. Although she was some sixty yards or so away from me, I could clearly hear that she was singing to herself. Obviously convinced that she was alone, the volume of the song grew and she began to dance, skipping erratically in circles. I was reminded of the old posters, showing a dancing fisherman resplendent in sou'wester and sea boots, telling the reader that

'Skegness is so bracing'. Her dog, with an obvious appreciation of the occasion, bounced enthusiastically around her. What should I do? Declare my presence and embarrass her, or let her get on with her celebration of the evening and depart none the wiser that she had been observed? I sat as still as I could, willing her to go. Suddenly she completed a circle and came to an abrupt halt, staring in my direction. I could just make out her face, flushed with exertion, as her gaze travelled up the rungs of the high seat and on to me. She moved in closer, peering up with a dawning, horrified look of realisation, and finally spoke.

'Are you real?' she gasped. 'I'm afraid so', I replied. Not another word was exchanged. The poor woman fled.

There have been some truly worrying experiences as well. One seat, built more in hope than judgement against a rather thin poplar, swayed so badly in the light wind that I spent the first hour in it feeling terrified. The terror later gave way to seasickness instead. It's a good job that no deer showed itself that morning – I couldn't have taken a shot even if I'd felt the platform was steady enough. It was a huge relief to climb down at the end, even if the prospect of a full fried breakfast at the farmhouse was no longer quite so appealing as it had been earlier.

I remember also being shown to another seat, made of larch poles fixed crudely together with six-inch nails and propped against a tree, with no attempt at any kind of reinforcement or wiring. I pointed out that one of the bottom ladder rungs was broken. 'You'll be all right', my host reassured me, 'just try not to put your weight in the centre when you climb up'. Too young and foolish to disagree, I had visions of a Buster-Keaton-style descent, with rung after rung snapping beneath me, as I made my nervous way to the top.

An impressive, newly constructed box seat – imagine a small cabin on stilts – was to be my home for another sit out. The owner was certainly proud of it. 'Last for ever', he said, patting one of the telegraph poles supporting it. And it was certainly a pleasure to be in, roomy and warm on a cold February evening. You could have got half a dozen people in there comfortably, the seats were cushioned, a rifle rack stood against the wall and there were even holders provided for thermos flasks and lunch boxes. I joked about it just needing a television and microwave. 'Working on it, mate, working on it', he told me cheerfully. I spent a very enjoyable few hours in this paragon, shooting two does which were gralloched suspended on the cross bar provided for that very purpose between two of the supports.

Another guest and I swapped locations for the morning stalk; I went to sit on the other side of the estate whilst he was directed to the box seat. It must have been a bit blowy during the night. All he found was the four support poles, still concreted firmly vertical and supporting a bare platform, surrounded by the sad, scattered remains of the rest of the box. I think that it's been left that way ever since.

It's not all bad though. A fondly remembered high seat session takes me back to Norfolk, this time in a lean-to seat against a lone tree overlooking a grassy bowl. I can't remember a thing about the seat itself, which means that at least it must have been safe. What I can remember is that it was a good year for wild raspberries and I had cut a couple of canes and hooked them over a branch to provide sustenance through the vigil. My pocket radio, through a single earpiece, provided me with a Blondie concert as an unnecessary but enjoyable distraction.

The evening was still and warm, and to top it all there was no shortage of deer. As I enjoyed the berries, I could see two sets of roe does with twin kids feeding away to either side of me, the kids occasionally bursting into games of chase or kicking out with their hind legs and running around in circles for no better reason than the sheer joy of it. A roe buck, far too good to shoot, wandered in from one side and couched in full view only a few yards from where I was sitting. I didn't have my camera with me, but it didn't really matter – it was good just to be there and watch. In the near distance, a huge Norfolk red stag made a brief appearance on the woodline before ghosting out of sight and I could have sworn that I saw a Chinese water deer picking its way unobtrusively through the long grass. A small herd of fallow does, dappled in their summer coats, completed the picture in the far fields. All I needed now was the muntjac for which I had come.

There are times when it seems as though there's nothing better than sitting and watching the world go about its business around you. As the

Blondie concert came to an end and the final bars of 'Heart of Glass' faded away, the light was finally beginning to fail when, as if on cue, a big muntjac buck stepped out of the trees to one side of me. It was almost with reluctance that I added him to the cull, as it seemed a shame to bring such a perfect evening to a close.

Hit or Miss?

A timely reminder to trust your instincts – and your dog

Sometimes we see what our brains tell us we want to see, rather than encouraging us to trust our instincts and apply a sound dollop of common sense. Certainly this is true of deer stalking, and I'm probably as guilty as the next man. If you are wondering what on earth I'm going on about, the following story might just give you an idea.

An early morning visit to my Hampshire stalking patch had proved fruitless thus far. I had had a few frustrating glimpses of what might have been shootable roe in dense cover, plus one young spiker, skylined magnificently on a grassy mound and well within range but without a backstop for the bullet. And, to top it all, I had also spotted two fallow prickets caught 'bang to rights' grazing like cattle in a meadow, with all conditions perfect for a shot or even two, were it not for the fact that open season was still a couple of weeks away. A magnificent roebuck, well into medal class, patrolling his territory in preparation for the impending rut had briefly raised my spirits, but an animal of his quality wasn't on the cull agenda for today. It looked as though the morning was going to turn out to be a blank.

Heading back towards the car now, and perhaps not moving as carefully as I should have been, the foliage on one side opened out suddenly to allow me to see some fifty yards into the woods. The little muntjac buck and I saw each other at the same time: both of us froze instantly. Perhaps he had only caught my movement and didn't identify me as an immediate threat, but instead of bolting for cover he stayed where he was and stared at me. A few yards behind him and to his right a second muntjac – I never really discovered what sex it was, although later events offered a suggestion – fed on, unaware of the drama, with only its back showing above the line of a fallen tree.

The moment was not going to last forever. As slowly and as smoothly as I could, I slid the rifle off my shoulder and onto the double sticks. Amazingly, the muntjac carried on staring at me and still didn't move. As soon as the cross hairs floated onto his shoulder I released the shot. The buck took off like a rocket and disappeared into the nearby cover. The second animal had also decided, unsurprisingly, that it was time to be somewhere else and was nowhere to be seen.

Many people will tell you that muntjac should always drop to a well-placed shot, but this isn't always the case, especially when you are using a fast, small bullet like the 100 grain loads that I prefer for use in the .243. I have taken everything up to red deer stags with them and find that they kill just as efficiently as a larger bullet. What they do lack, however, is the terminal energy to knock a deer down on the spot, especially one already poised for flight, which is why I favour a heavier calibre for larger deer. The animal might be clinically dead but, especially if it is already poised for flight, a primitive flight reflex can still propel the body a short distance before everything shuts down. Whatever the case, I wasn't surprised by this reaction and confidently expected to find a heavy blood trail and a dead animal very close by.

If you can't see where a shot deer has dropped, it's always a good idea to wait a few minutes before moving in. If the animal has not expired, it may still have enough strength to get up and dash off rather than expire quietly, and as a bonus something else may appear. So I simply watched for a while, rifle still on the sticks and ready to fire again if need be.

After about five minutes there was no sign of any activity so I carefully approached the spot where the buck had been standing. Against all expectations, there was nothing to show any signs of a bullet strike on the buck beyond a few hairs, and I really had to search for these. A good 'engine room' shot to the heart and lung area should have left a large amount of blood and tissue, but even getting down on hands and knees and running my hands across the damp woodland floor yielded nothing. Had I just imagined a clean shot? I thought not – everything had felt good – but there was nothing here to support that. With a sinking heart I decided that I had to expect the grim outcome of a broken leg or similar. The few hairs that I had found could not, sadly, allow me to assume a clean miss.

Rather than contaminate any scent trail by trying to follow it myself, I made my way back to the car and collected the spaniel. A springer may not be the ideal deer dog but Mole, having proven herself many times in practice and a few in earnest, knew immediately what was expected of her, put her nose to the ground and there was no doubt that she was finding something interesting. After investigating the immediate area where the buck had been standing when hit, she set off, nose still glued to the ground and tail moving at double the normal speed, in the direction it had taken. So far, all the signs were encouraging that we might yet rectify the situation. I was about to stop her and put the long tracking lead on (I didn't want her mixing it with a perhaps lightly wounded muntjac buck in cover – I've seen the damage that these seemingly innocuous little deer can inflict with their canine tusks) when I became aware of a muntjac moving off to one side of us.

Was it moving normally? I couldn't tell, but unusually it stopped and looked back at man and dog. By this point the rifle was in my shoulder and supported by a convenient tree. With only head and neck showing as the buck looked back over its shoulder at us through the light vegetation, I could see the shot was safe and took it. The muntjac was felled instantly by the bullet to the base of its neck, kicked a couple of times and lay still.

Keen to see where the original shot had gone, I approached the deer to find… nothing. There were no wound marks at all, apart from the one to the neck. At this point the doubts and self-delusion started, mainly because I wanted to convince myself that this was the original animal and that any potential problem had been cleared up. It was a small buck, and I had originally shot at a small buck. It had been moving strangely, hadn't it? And surely no healthy muntjac would have stopped to look back at a man and a dog a mere twenty yards or so away when it had been disturbed from cover? As I moved to gralloch the animal, against all my better instincts I was persuading myself that this was the one.

Out of the corner of my eye, I became aware that the dog was still working. Normally at this point she is all attention in the knowledge that something tasty is about to come her way as a reward for her efforts. Now, however, she still had her nose to the ground on a totally different line to the one that the dead buck in front of me had taken. Intrigued, I followed her and found the original muntjac, stone dead to a high heart shot, about twenty yards into the low bramble.

If many years of stalking deer have taught me one thing, it is never to make assumptions about them: yet it's a lesson that I still occasionally forget. That, perhaps, is the attraction of deer to me – no matter how much you think you may know, there is always a new experience just around the corner. For me also, this episode reinforced a serious point that we all ought to consider. A dog that is capable of reliably following a blood trail is invaluable, whether it stalks with you or remains in the car as an 'insurance policy'. All stalkers should at least have access to such a dog, even if it belongs to a friend who can be called upon to come and help if needed.

Had it not been for Mole, that first buck would probably still be lying there today, a waste of good venison and, perhaps even more important for my own peace of mind, a lingering doubt over the one that might have got away.

The Pig

Recalling the pursuit of an unusually large muntjac buck

Of his kind, he was the largest that I personally have ever seen, although I have heard of larger. Certainly he stood out as an exceptional specimen. He lived in an oasis of broadleaf and scrub that took up a few hundred acres in the middle of some extensive hedged farmland. This stalking patch was an attractive refuge to the few local roe and wandering herds of fallow, but to the muntjac, amongst which the Pig was the undoubted king, it was the only suitable habitat for miles.

Nobody knew where he came from. Suddenly he simply turned up, larger than life – it was not as though he was a particularly big, already known buck that had noticeably become huge as he matured. He quickly earned the nickname 'Pig' when the three of us who shared the stalking became aware of his presence. His name was perhaps inevitable given his size and the porcine shape of a muntjac. He was certainly old, with very short pedicles but carrying exceptional antlers for his species, and he quickly became a sort of grail to us, and the source of an undeclared competition as to who would catch up with him first.

Catching up with the Pig did not, however, prove to be easy. Perhaps you don't get to be that size by being stupid when you are a deer in an actively stalked landscape. Over the two years I knew him, I only ever once saw him away from cover. For the rest of the time he was a tantalisingly fleeting shape among the brambles and hazel coppice.

If cats have nine lives, goodness knows how many the Pig had. One of us nearly caught up with him one early morning, as he sauntered down a narrow ride seemingly without a care in the world. The shot, from a high seat, would have been simple at an unchallenging fifty yards or so. With the rifle steadily rested on the front bar of the seat, all that was needed was for the Pig to take a few more paces to step clear of a low hanging branch and allow for a clear shot. With the branch between him and the shooter he suddenly stopped and stood stock still, for what the observer felt was something like two minutes, broadside on but just obscured by the branch. Then, for no reason whatsoever, the Pig simply hopped off the side of the track and disappeared, and that was that.

Shortly afterwards I found myself in the same seat. It was another early morning in late autumn and the leaf cover was disappearing fast so visibility was good compared to the almost tropical foliage of the summer months. I had been there for a good hour, enjoying the light coming up and the passage of various birds and animals about their business. Around me were a few small islands of low bramble, most of them no more than a few square feet in size, big enough to break up the ground but not so large as to obscure it completely, and with fair amounts of clear space around each one. As I watched a melanistic pheasant scratching about in the woodland floor just below me, a glorious reflection of unexpected colours among his black plumage in the streaming sunlight, I became aware of movement out of the corner of my eye and a small muntjac doe made her way cautiously towards one of the bramble patches some thirty yards from me. As she stopped to look behind her, my shot dropped her instantly.

I reloaded and watched for movement. It was clear that the shot had killed her instantly so, rather than dismount and conduct the gralloch, I decided to sit and wait for another half-hour in case something else turned up. Eventually I climbed down and approached the doe. As I did so, from the brambles she had been making for – a patch, mind, of no more than the footprint of an estate car and a couple of feet in height – erupted the Pig, tail vertical and travelling flat out. There was no way he could have approached the brambles unseen while I was in the seat so he must have been there the whole time, watching me climb up in the half-light of dawn, through the shot and my subsequent wait. And all this time I had had no idea of his presence.

He was saved later that winter by an unexpected bout of buck fever, when one of us had a better than fair chance of a clear shot at short range when, out of the blue, the stalker got the shakes. This was a man who had been stalking for almost twenty years and had shot countless muntjac in his time. 'I just went to pieces', he said afterwards, amid a few well-chosen expletives. 'Couldn't understand it, hasn't happened for years. Snatched the trigger and pulled the shot. Even saw the bullet strike in the track, a good six inches over the top of his shoulder.'

It became clear to us all that the Pig must have a charmed life. He was shot at and inexplicably missed at least once more to my certain knowledge, and he was totally unforgiving if his stalker made the slightest error of wind or footfall. At other times he was just pure lucky. One encounter at last light proved impossible as, despite a clear picture in the binoculars, the shooter just couldn't find him in the riflescope. On another occasion the keeper turned up to fill the pheasant hoppers in the final stages of a stalk, moving him away, fairly unconcerned, from browsing beside a release pen. The Pig was so adept at disappearing where there seemed to be no cover that we began to joke uneasily that he climbed trees and hid down rabbit holes. It seemed that the beast was destined to die not from a bullet, but from either old age or a heart attack brought on by laughing at our efforts.

I am afraid to report that the Pig eventually met his end, like so many high quality muntjac bucks, virtually by accident. A morning sit out overlooking a sizeable glade which was attractive to the fallow had proven fruitless; although early October, the sun had come up hot in a cloudless sky and it was promising to be a beautiful day. Convinced that nothing was going to show now, I decided to pack up, and made ready to climb down from the seat. Halfway down the ladder, with rifle unloaded and bolt back in its pouch, I happened to glance over my shoulder and saw the Pig step out of the tree line and start to cross the far end of the glade. There was no time for subtlety. Inexplicably he did not seem to see me scramble back up into the seat, nor hear me refit the bolt, reload and chamber a round. By the time I was ready to shoot he was just a few yards from the opposite tree line, about to step into cover and safety.

He clearly wasn't going to stop so there was nothing for it but to call a sharp 'Oi!' and hope he'd pause and look back rather than do the sensible thing and disappear. To my near disbelief he actually made a mistake and stopped, three quarters on to me, and the rifle seemed to go off on its own.

There he lay, a real monster, later weighing in at a larder weight of 37 pounds compared to the 28 pounds I'd normally expect a good average buck to come in at. And as for his head: well, trophies aren't everything, but even with a malform to one antler (he must have taken a knock whilst in velvet) he still managed to achieve a very comfortable gold CIC ranking. Was I right to have removed him from the patch? Some might argue that as a big, dominant buck he might have acted as a 'policeman', keeping out the lesser bucks as a strong territorial roe might. But it was clear from his pedicle length that he was getting old and in addition to this one of his canine tusks was broken; this in itself would have been enough to take the edge off his mastery.

It would be tempting to say that I shall not see his like again but as far as muntjac are concerned – never say never! Unlike a good roe buck whose habits can be marked down, a quality muntjac is more often than not taken by pure chance. For now the Pig remains a lifetime best and I am grateful that I was granted the good fortune finally to catch up with him – even if, to this day, I remain unforgiven by my fellow stalkers for my sheer luck.

The Roe Rut

In search of rutting roe deer

It had been a strange roe rut in this particular year. I don't usually expect to see much real activity here in Hampshire until the last week in July, and it then tends to go on for a week or ten days into August before finally petering out. It was very surprising, then, to receive a phone call from my stalking partner telling me that the rut was already in full swing by mid-July. It could have been something to do with the very untypically hot summer conditions we had experienced earlier in the month but, by the time I could finally get out, the rut, though certainly taking place on my own patch, seemed to be running in fits and starts rather than the full-on affair that we normally hope to see.

As July turned into August, work pressures finally eased off and I set out to see what was about and hopefully account for one or two cull animals. The rut is an excellent time to get a good look at your mature bucks, which can be elusive throughout the rest of the year. When the urge to breed overtakes them they become rather less cautious and easier to see, making the job of selecting which ones should join the cull plan much simpler.

It was warm with a cooling light breeze as I arrived on the patch for the evening session. Sadly the hot, heavy and humid atmosphere that had threatened thunderstorms the previous day had cleared: a shame, as this kind of weather is generally considered to be the best for encouraging rutting activity. Still, I set off with high hopes, planning to walk, stalk and hopefully call in an animal or two rather than sit in a high seat.

There seemed to be does everywhere, but ominously many seemed to be accompanied only by their kids. This was a bad sign. What I really wanted to see were lone does that had left their kids somewhere safe before going off to entice a buck onto their chosen rutting ground, offering a chance to call in a buck by imitating them, or bringing in a doe already accompanied by a buck by using a kid's alarm call.

A small piece of new clear fell, about half the size of a football field, looked promising. At one end of it a lone doe fed quietly alongside the main tree line, and I settled down to watch her and see if she was actually alone. After a few minutes I thought that I'd try to draw her closer with a few kid *fieps*, but the result was not what I had expected. Although her head went up, another lone doe appeared from behind us and approached hesitantly to within a few yards before identifying me and going off barking. The original doe remained where she was, but seemed to be watching something intently away to another side. Soon what looked like a buck emerged and stood within a short distance of her. I couldn't make out its antlers properly, but there seemed to be some small growth on its head – an old buck who had 'gone back', perhaps? If so, he would be an ideal candidate to join the cull.

Something felt wrong, though, and my suspicions increased as the 'buck' was joined by a small kid with which it was clearly in company. I looked in vain for a pizzle on the animal but couldn't see one, and concluded that this was an old doe that had produced some rudimentary antler growth as they occasionally do. Shooting her would have been a disastrous mistake, leaving an orphaned dependent kid, and a good reminder to identify your target carefully before you shoot and not to leap to conclusions.

Finally, a genuine buck appeared, in company with a doe that he was clearly interested in if not actively pursuing. As he was not particularly big, either in terms of body or antler size, he was certainly takeable. There was a complication though. By this point there were half a dozen roe in full view so I dared not move, and could only watch in frustration as he and his doe moved off slowly, screened by a hawthorn bush in the only direction that blocked any possible shot. He proved to be the last buck I saw that evening.

Calling over the next hour produced only does, some of which came in at full speed, but no bucks. I was beginning to wonder if the rut had finished as early as it had started.

To be on the ground at first light the next morning meant a 3am start. Whilst getting up so early is always hard, it's certainly worth it to be there when the sun comes up. I decided to move through the woods to the corner of a large field and try some calling to see what might turn up. There was no need; a pair of roe was already there, grazing unconcernedly on the clover among the short grass. I recognised the buck as one of the patch's 'bruisers', a big-bodied animal with antlers that would certainly have made at least a silver medal, so I decided to leave him in peace. He and the doe, another noticeably large deer, eventually moved off around the corner and I carefully edged up the wood line towards the point where they had disappeared.

Halfway there, I spotted the unmistakeable rump of a roe protruding from behind a bush. Had the two animals decided to come back onto the field? Just in case I got the rifle up onto the sticks, just in time, as the animal, a small doe and certainly not the one which had just left, came into full view and stared at me. There was a buck with her, now just visible behind the bush. The doe stared at me, then went through the typical roe pantomime of pretending to put her head down to feed before whipping it back up to stare again. The buck moved out to stand behind her, a very average six pointer which was certainly fair game, but could I get a shot?

As is so often the case in these circumstances it was the doe who took the lead and, despite not being sure what the strange object in front of her was, decided that it was time to leave and led the buck off across the field. It was time for desperate measures; as they were not in full flight, a sharp whistle persuaded them to stop and look back for long enough to get an aimed shot away.

The bullet took the buck across the top of the heart. He leapt forward and collapsed, while the doe made off, this time at full speed. He lay still in full view; I watched carefully for a while, but a cautious approach and a tap on the eyeball with the end of the stalking stick confirmed that the shot had been instantly fatal. A nearby tree provided a branch to perform a suspended gralloch and shade to hang the carcase in while I carried on, unsuccessfully, to look for another shootable buck before the sun signalled that it was time to stop for the morning.

I went home well satisfied, with the welcome bonus of a fresh liver to form the centrepiece of a proper stalker's breakfast to share with a waking family – what better way to celebrate success, and to make up for such an early start?

Roe Liver

Roe liver is lightly textured and has a more delicate flavour than the calf or lamb's liver more usually available at the butcher's. A healthy liver should be a uniform dark brown all over with no discolouration. You seldom see it offered for sale as it has long, and rightly, been considered as the stalker's 'perks'.

The simplest way to cook it is probably the best; slice it into strips about half an inch thick, coat these lightly in flour and fry gently in some butter for a few minutes on each side. Accompanied by the kidneys along with some scrambled eggs and bacon, the liver melts in the mouth and makes a delicious breakfast for several hungry stalkers.

A Strange Meeting

It was around the time of the summer solstice, and my patch lay conveniently on the flightline of all the would-be druids, white witches and assorted earth children who flock annually to Stonehenge from the Home Counties to mark the event. At such times every sensible farmer in the district goes out of his way to block all possible access points with immovable farm machinery or ditches, to prevent the arrival of travellers or illegal 'raves'.

My stalking grounds were no different. At the entrance to the track I found a hulking pile of very imaginative rusty ironwork that would have held back Genghis Khan and the Mongol hordes, never mind Swampy and a few of his mates. As a result I had to leave the Land Rover next to it and walk in, rather than drive down and park up in my usual spot. I very much hoped that tonight would not be the night that I struck too lucky among the deer population. I don't mind lugging the occasional yearling about, but I don't get the pleasure that I used to out of yomping two or three miles with a big buck on my back. If hares double their weight in every mile that they are carried, I'm prepared to swear that roe quadruple theirs.

Anyway, I eventually got to the Big Wood and started down the main ride. Coming round a bend, I found an unexpected visitor. Kneeling at the base of a tree was a girl in her late teens, hands clasped on her lap and with a serene expression indicating deep fulfilment on her face. She was dressed in an old parka jacket, bright red boots and a rather fetching hat with green pom-poms that I suspected she had collected in the course of mugging an unsuspecting elf. A fine layer of dust – possibly *Côtes de A303* – completed the ensemble.

She was entirely oblivious to my presence. I broke rudely into her reverie with a quiet cough and asked her what she was doing in the middle of a very large, and very private, estate.

To be fair, I didn't mean to startle her, but the sudden appearance of an armed and masked (I'd forgotten that I had it on) stranger, dressed in finest Disruptive Pattern Material, must have been a touch unsettling. She eventually regained her composure and announced in a sweet, dreamy voice that she wanted 'to be with the trees'. I've come across a few odd things whilst out and about but now I'd met a genuine tree hugger – a bit of a first for me at the time. From her spaced-out demeanour and a dodgy-looking cigarette stub on the ground beside her, I suspected that she was rather keen on other plants as well.

I gently explained that the land was private and that she really shouldn't be there, helpfully pointing out the best way back to the main road and some rather more accessible trees for her to be with. She started to leave and then, as an afterthought, asked who I was. Several unworthy thoughts crossed my mind, but instead I identified myself and foolishly let slip that I was the local deer manager.

She considered this for a moment. 'What do you do?' she asked.

Being an intuitive soul, I knew that a sensitive approach to the answer was required. I explained that I kept an eye on the deer and looked after them as best I could. Showing considerable perception for one so young she pointed to the rifle on my shoulder. 'What's that for, then?'

I instinctively felt that a full explanation would not go down well. Instead, I hedged a bit and suggested that occasionally a deer might have to be put out of its misery, say after being hit by a car. All traces of cheerful dreaminess left her face. I'll swear that she grew a couple of inches as the Awful Truth sank in and she stiffened with indignation.

'You kill them!' she spat at me. 'You horrible person, you...' I really cannot bring myself to repeat some of the more choice expressions that followed, but any self-respecting squaddie would have been proud. Shall we just say that not only did she reveal a few hitherto unknown facts about my lineage, but that I also learned an innovative use for my rifle not specified within the conditions on the FAC. I got the distinct impression that our relationship was doomed.

She paused for breath, and sought the right words to conclude our little chat. '*You, you...*' She paused as she searched for the right word. 'You *ugly* man!' she concluded, with a triumphant if not entirely attractive screech and a flourish of her arms. Decisively denying me any further opportunity for philosophical discussion she snatched up a bedding roll, slung it furiously over one shoulder and departed at speed. I was pleased to note that she was heading in the right direction for Stonehenge and all points west.

I'm sure that the trees miss her.

The Twins

Recalling a series of frustrating encounters
with a pair of yearling roe bucks

I always feel that it's important to get cracking on the roe buck cull the moment the season opens on the first of April. Not shooting the big bucks, mind – they come later – but what a lot of people like to term 'cull bucks', the yearlings and two-year-olds that form the greater part of any management plan aimed at a well-balanced roe population. These younger animals can be relatively easy to stalk as they don't have the wariness and experience of their older counterparts, but it's easy to forget that as spring progresses and the older bucks protect their territories ever more jealously, the lesser animals spend more and more time avoiding them. The result of this increased timidity is that they can often become all-but invisible to the stalker by early summer.

By the middle of April in the year in question I was already beginning to see some mature roe in hard horn and clean of their velvet, that temporary furry covering to the growing antler. This is not the case with the youngsters, who are inevitably behind in the annual antler cycle; it's not unusual to be finding these still cleaning their new headgear well into June.

I first became aware of the two young roe bucks in question during an early season drive around the patch at the beginning of April. I like to do this whenever I have time, normally after an early morning stalking session, just to see what is about and build up a picture in my own head of where I should be directing my efforts. I prefer not to shoot from the vehicle on these occasions even though it is now legal (as long as the vehicle is stationary and the engine switched off). This is not down to any form of purism – it's just that I appreciate the deer standing so that I can have a good look at them through the binoculars. If I feel a need to shoot I'll generally drive round the corner, park up and stalk back on foot. Once deer have come to associate road vehicles with danger they are usually away like a shot the moment one appears – a useful indicator in itself that someone else may be up to no good.

The two small bucks were feeding only about forty metres off the track as I halted the little Suzuki. They watched me with mild interest as I studied them through the binoculars out of the car window, relaxed enough to put their heads down and snip a piece of some tempting new growth between stares. Both were typical yearling roe, with slim, light, leggy bodies and thin necks, still in full winter coat, neither of them anything special to look at and both ideal additions to the buck cull. Their antlers, such as they were, consisted of no more than an inch or so of velvet-covered growth, which clearly had some way to go. I marked them down as twins from the previous year although there was no sign of a mature doe with them – presumably she had either become a statistic in the cull plan a month or two previously, or fallen victim to the main road on our boundary. Eventually the pair moved off, showing no real alarm, just taking a gentle trot into the woods, leaving me mentally noting them as subjects for closer attention with a rifle in due course.

Work demands meant that I wasn't able to get onto the ground for the next few days, but Saturday morning was clear and first light found me ready to go. The wind was perfect for the corner where I had last seen the two small bucks, so this seemed to be as good a place to start as any. The foliage had not yet started to thicken out on the woodland floor so I had decent visibility for at least a hundred metres through the trees in all directions, and a grassy footpath gave me easy quiet progress. Stopping to glass around me every few paces, I quickly picked up a roe feeding quietly. As I watched, a second stepped out from behind a tree to join it. From their build and undeveloped antlers I could see that these were the two yearlings from earlier in the week.

Despite the lack of any real ground cover to speak of, there were still too many obstructions to allow a shot from where I was so I decided to close the range and look for a clear line. A large clump of brambles provided me with plenty of cover to move round unobserved by the deer and I was confident of success. In fact, with a sound moderator and provided the deer had not seen me by the time I took the first shot, I had every expectation of collecting both of them.

A short crawl from the brambles stood an ancient oak, which would provide plenty of cover for me to get to my feet, set the rifle on the double sticks and ease myself around the trunk ready to shoot. However, fifty metres away, where the deer should have been, there was… nothing. In the few minutes it had taken me to move into a shooting position they had simply disappeared. The wind was perfect and, as far as I was aware, they hadn't suspected my presence. Had something else disturbed them, or had they simply decided to move on? There's no way of knowing, but that was the last I saw of them that morning. It wasn't an issue as there would be other chances and the morning wasn't a washout anyway. Only half-an-hour later I encountered a lone fallow pricket: a welcome cull opportunity with the close season only a few weeks off.

I didn't come across the Twins (as I had now started to think of them) again until a fortnight later, when I saw them out feeding on a small grass meadow about half-an-hour before last light. Once again, the set-up was perfect for a simple stalk along the wood edge with a dry ditch to allow me a final approach. I emerged from the ditch to see a deer rump disappearing into the wood line on the other side of the meadow. At least I had the consolation of knowing that it hadn't been me that had sent the Twins packing, as a large dog fox was sitting staring in my direction, and I'll swear that he was grinning, a few yards from where the deer had been a moment before. Clearly his presence had made them uncomfortable enough to decamp. To rub salt into the wound, he didn't even hang around long enough for me to get a shot.

A week or so passed and I came across the two brothers again, this time chasing each other around in play, as young deer often do, through a scrubby area not far from our previous encounters. This time all I had to do was set my rifle onto the sticks and wait for them to emerge from behind a few small bushes. All they had to do was carry on in the direction they had been heading, turn right towards me, or turn back and I was in with a chance. True to form, however, they took the unseen path and that was that.

As the season progressed, I saw the Twins fairly regularly but no real opportunity to get close to them developed. They seemed content to stay together rather than split up and perhaps, subconsciously, I'd decided to give them best. It's not as though I was going through a lean stalking patch as happens from time to time. I was successful enough elsewhere, but it seemed that these two were simply not fated to join their fellows in the larder.

Eventually, with the roe rut fast approaching, we had what was to be our last meeting. There was nothing momentous about the occasion, no classic stalk or hair-raising sudden encounter, in fact it all came as something of an anti-climax. I was in their corner of the patch and about to gralloch a small muntjac doe which I'd caught crossing the meadow where the fox incident had occurred when, with rifle unloaded and resplendent in blue latex gloves, I suddenly became aware of a small roe stepping out of cover only a short distance away. Lying flat on the ground I refitted the magazine, chambered a round carefully and reached for the sticks. To gain a safe backstop the shot had to be taken standing but, as I prepared to raise myself slowly into a shooting position, the second Twin also came into view. Caught in the open and with nothing to conceal myself behind, there was no option but to try for it.

Amazingly, neither deer seemed to notice me rise to my feet. At the shot, the buck left standing simply took a couple of steps and looked around for the reason his companion had suddenly dropped. A second .308 bullet left the barrel and the whole business was over in seconds.

There was certainly nothing remarkable about the two yearling bucks. Their antlers, such as they were, comprised no more than a couple of short spikes, they were small compared to their contemporaries on the patch, and for all intents and purposes they might have been identical twins. Perfect cull bucks, but for some strange reason I couldn't help feeling a bit guilty that it was no more than dumb luck that finally allowed me to catch up with them.

Tales from Glen Garron

A Trout of Many Colours

Good deeds can occasionally be done in ignorance of the recipient

'Where's Ratchet, grandma?'

Lady Mary looked up fondly at the enquirer, the ten-year-old son of her eldest daughter, who was staying with his grandparents at Glen Garron whilst his parents took an extended African holiday. Edward was a studious, bespectacled lad who always looked as though he desperately needed a good meal, despite a prodigious appetite that Shuna the cook found his most appealing trait. Lady Mary put down her copy of *Country Life* and raised an eyebrow.

'I think it's in London, darling, but why do you ask?'

'Well,' Edward regarded her seriously, as he considered his reply with deliberate care. 'Willie said this morning that he thought my casting keeps "gaun tae ratchet". The last three words were delivered in an excellent imitation of Willie Cameron's Highland burr.

Lady Mary sighed. She really would have to speak with the head stalker, who had been charged with teaching young Edward to cast a fly and then catching his first trout from one of the many small hill lochs on the estate. Edward clearly worshipped his mentor and hung on his every word, but she couldn't send him home with some of Willie's choicer phrases. Across the drawing room of the Lodge there was a suppressed snort of laughter from behind *The Daily Telegraph*; it was obvious that the Colonel had no intention of getting involved in this one.

The Colonel, in fact, had other worries. Someone was poaching the roe and red deer from the road edges of the estate forestry. Unexplained grallochs, often with the heads and legs of out-of-season animals, had been found left in ditches, and the deer themselves, normally so relaxed about motor vehicles, were now noticeably shying away from any that appeared near them. Willie and his son, Archie, accompanied by the Colonel himself, had spent many hours staking out likely spots, but they couldn't be everywhere at once and so far the poacher had proven elusive.

Worse yet, they had a pretty good idea of who was responsible – a local sheep farmer who ran a small pheasant shoot further down the glen. 'A damn'd flying chicken and woolly maggot man' Willie dismissively called him, betraying his thinly disguised contempt both for game-birds lower down the pecking order than his beloved grouse and for the sheep that strayed onto the moors, destroying precious heather in the process. 'Ach, and he's a Macdonald intae the bargain. Ah'd like to banjo the yahoo if I could just catch him at it.' Lady Mary was more worried about the Colonel. No longer a young man, he took events in the glen to heart and she could see that he was becoming preoccupied; his manner, normally good-humoured, had become distracted of late and dark rings around his eyes betrayed a lack of sleep. Attempts to persuade him to leave matters to the stalkers were ineffectual.

Willie Cameron was more concerned about getting young Edward his first trout. He was a clever lad with a bright and enquiring mind, way ahead of his classmates, and Willie liked him enormously. The boy had a special gift for electronics and took delight in constructing clever devices such as a burglar alarm for his bedroom and a motion-activated spray to keep the local heron from the fish pool in the Lodge garden. However, as he cheerfully admitted, he was no good at sports of any kind. The problem was that the lad had no coordination; the timing of a simple overhead cast seemed beyond him, and their sessions practising on the manicured lawn of the Lodge with a simple tuft of wool in the place of a fly (Willie shuddered at the thought of such a sharp object careering backwards and forwards out of control) had so far resulted in some truly Gordian tangles. He despaired of getting Edward to the point where he could deceive a brown trout when only a few weeks of his holiday remained. After weeks of struggling, maybe one cast in ten might fly true; the remainder were horrible, splashy disasters that would scare off any self-respecting wild trout in the vicinity.

Over a pint at the Kelpie Inn that night, a preoccupied Willie discussed the problem with his son. Archie thought about it for a moment. 'Hang on, Da' he said. 'Doesn't Jack Fraser owe you a favour or two?' Quickly he explained what he had in mind. Willie nodded slowly and his face gradually brightened. 'Aye, d'ye know, that just might be it. I'll give him a call.'

Back at the Lodge, Lady Mary and Edward were sitting alone watching a gardening programme on the television. The Colonel had gone out for another vigil on the roadside hoping to catch the poacher, and Lady Mary knew that he would not return until the small hours. She pointed at the screen. 'Is it easy to make one of those?' she asked Edward, who assured her that it was, given the right parts. She told him why, and together they went to the computer to place an order. Time passed and Edward's casting made little improvement, but Willie seemed pleased with his protégé's progress, offering enthusiastic encouragement and declaring that it would soon be time to try for a trout. 'Maybe even tomorrow,' he said, before leaving to arrange a rendezvous with Jack Fraser. Later that day he guided Jack's van along a small dirt track leading up the hill, to make a very special delivery.

At around the same time the postman delivered something entirely different, this time contained in a small parcel, to Glen Garron Lodge and marked for the personal attention of Lady Mary. That night, while Willie, Archie and the Colonel were out on another fruitless poacher watch, two figures slipped out of the Lodge and drove off, their destination a darkened farmyard. In the morning an excited Edward, bearing his eight-foot fly rod, accompanied Willie and the Colonel to a small hill loch in the hills overlooking the Lodge. It was a long trudge through the heather and Willie deliberately made a circuitous approach, assuring his companions that it would put the wind right for easier casting. The Colonel was surprised at the choice of venue, which he'd written off as a fishing spot long ago, but trusted Willie's judgement. He also wondered why they had not driven up but decided that this was Willie's way of creating more of an occasion. The loch was not big, its area covering little more than two tennis courts, but Willie assured them that it held fish. 'Though it's up to ye to catch them,' he told Edward seriously.

He tied a fly onto the leader. 'Off ye go lad.' Edward took his stance, started to cast, and promptly hooked a tuft of heather behind him. 'Never ye mind, lad, try again,' Willie encouraged him. The next attempt, helped by the breeze from behind Edward's back, saw the line make it out across the water to land like a linear brick. Edward twitched the fly back sheepishly as Willie had instructed him: nothing happened.

Ten minutes later the water had been thoroughly whipped and the Colonel was starting to look worried, but Willie was confident. He announced that it was time to try a dry fly, and, with his back to the rest of the party, opened his pocket flybox and bent over the line. 'There ye go,' he said, mentally crossing his fingers for luck. 'Cast it straight out.'

This time the line sailed out and landed with a soft plop. 'It's a dry, no need to move it,' Willie announced. The three of them watched the small spot in the surface of the water and, to their surprise and delight, saw it engulfed by an emerging mouth. 'Strike lad, strike!'

Edward lifted the rod, which bucked in his hand; a few minutes later a deep-bodied silver trout of about three quarters of a pound slid into the net, fielded expertly by the Colonel. Willie despatched and unhooked the fish and the three of them admired it as it lay in the heather. 'Whit a wee brammer!' Willie exclaimed. 'But isn't that a...' the Colonel started to say, before being silenced by a wink from Willie. '... rather good fish,' he concluded lamely. He paused and regarded Willie gravely for a moment, then nodded and smiled. 'A celebratory supper at the Lodge tonight, I think,' he announced. 'Willie, bring your good lady and young Archie along. Edward can eat his first trout as the main course.'

Willie passed on the good news when he got home. 'So it worked then?' asked Archie.

'Like a wee dream' came the answer. 'Though it must be the first time a fish has been seen in that shilpit loch for many a year. We'll have some sport out of it now, mind, it's fair stowed oot.' He took the flybox out of his pocket and opened it; a waiting terrier eagerly snapped up the high protein pellets that dropped to the ground.

As the celebration took place in the Lodge that evening, Geordie Macdonald cruised the main road through the estate in his battered pickup truck, cab windows open. He'd been concentrating his poaching efforts elsewhere for a while to let the heat in Glen Garron cool off, and had spent the previous night in Inverness at a long planned old comrades' reunion. Tonight, though, he knew that there was no danger of being caught. A chance meeting in the village shop with Shuna the cook had informed him that all his antagonists would be out of the way. The moderated rifle at his side was loaded and ready, and he was confident that the morning would see half a dozen fresh carcases ready for dropping off with a dealer contact who asked no questions.

He caught movement at the side of the road and switched on the searchlight on the cab roof. A roe buck stared back briefly but, instead of being transfixed by the beam, skipped quickly into the trees. Geordie cursed under his breath and drove on again. A few hundred yards later the same thing happened again. In fact, that night not one deer stood for long enough to allow him a shot and he went home empty-handed for the first time in a great many outings. In a year or so Geordie Macdonald would discover the small black box wired to his car battery and wonder what it was. In the meantime he couldn't work out why the farm cats shunned him, his sheep were skittish when he drove the fields delivering feed, and even his lurcher, usually such a good traveller, wouldn't settle whenever it was in the pickup. Sometimes he couldn't even persuade it to get in at all.

As of that moment though, and to the perplexed but very great relief of the Colonel, Glen Garron's poaching problems, not to mention those of the surrounding areas, inexplicably ceased.

A MIXED BAG OF TRIVIA

The challenge of achieving a Macnab – stalking a stag, shooting a brace of grouse and landing a salmon in a single day – has its origins in John Buchan's 1925 novel *John Macnab*. In the story, three successful but bored gentlemen set themselves the task of poaching two stags and a salmon (there are no grouse involved) from their neighbours' estates. To make the task even more difficult they forewarn the owners of their intentions in a letter signed simply 'John Macnab'.

The Field magazine hosts a Macnab Club, which offers a variety of alternative challenges to the classic Macnab of stag, salmon and grouse. Amongst others, these include:

- *Real Macnab – a stag and a salmon on the fly, 'poached' from a landowner who has accepted the challenge*
- *Southern Macnab – roebuck, sea trout and a couple of snipe*
- *MacMarsh – fallow buck, pike and a foreshore goose*
- *MacVermin – an 'impressive' rat, chalk stream pike and a brace of magpies*
- *MacScandi – moose, capercaillie and a trout on the fly*

Any one of these challenges has to be completed in a day, appropriately witnessed, and 'undertaken in a sporting and gentlemanly fashion'.

The surname Hartley derives from the words *hart*, a male deer, and *leah*, a meadow or pasture. In the same way, Raleigh translates as 'roe deer meadow'. Forenames Oprah and Elaine are taken from the Hebrew and Welsh respectively, both meaning fawn, and Oscar derives from the Gaelic Osgar, *os* meaning deer and *cara* lover, hence 'deer lover'.

In Roman myth, the young hunter Actaeon was transformed into a deer by Diana, the goddess of hunting, for daring to spy on her and her female companions while they bathed. He was subsequently torn to pieces by his own hunting dogs.

The Roman goddess Diana's equivalent in Greek mythology, Artemis, is credited with delaying the siege of Troy by controlling the weather to keep King Agamemnon's fleet harbour-bound as retribution for the killing of a sacred stag. Capturing another of her beloved animals, the Hind of Cyrenia, was one of the twelve labours set to Heracles (Hercules) by King Eurystheus. Artemis only allowed him to proceed with the task once he had promised to release the deer alive and unharmed after proving to the king that he had captured it.

Many ancient myths, such as the story of Romulus and Remus, involve children being raised by wild animals. Telephus, the illegitimate son of Heracles, was also abandoned to his fate as a newborn but suckled by a female deer until discovered by some shepherds. His name is taken from thele, *a teat, and* elaphus, *a deer.*

Buckfast, a village in Devon where the fortified wine of the same name is made, translates as 'the stronghold of the buck'.

Most people see Bambi as an American white-tailed deer thanks to the Walt Disney cartoon film. In the original Bambi: A Life in the Woods, *written by Austrian author Felix Salten in 1926, however, although we are not specifically told what species Bambi is, various clues suggest that he was a roe kid. The original book, by the way, is a charming, realistic and captivating read in which the animals only speak to allow the story to be told from their perspective. There is none of the later cuteness, and not a trace of Thumper the rabbit or Flower the skunk. The heavily anthropomorphic Disney adaptation bears very little resemblance to it.*

A red stag with twelve points to his antlers is commonly known as a Royal, and should possess 'all his rights', namely brow, bey and trey tines on each side as well as three top points. A fourteen pointer is less frequently referred to as an Imperial and a sixteen pointer as a Monarch. Tradition dictates that, to count as a true point, any protrusion from the main beam of the antler should be large enough to support a wedding ring. In earlier times it was a pocket watch, but the definition has changed as very few people carry those today.

The subject of Sir Edwin Landseer's famous painting, The Monarch of the Glen, though bearing six points to each antler, might not be considered as a true Royal by purists as neither set of top points form a cup capable of holding a glass of wine.

St Hubert is not the only saint associated with seeing a vision of a stag with a crucifix on its head resulting in his conversion to Christianity; both St Eustace and St Ignatius are credited with similar experiences.

Richmond Park in London, famous for its free-roaming red and fallow deer herds, was first enclosed as a royal hunting park by Charles I in 1637. The move was very unpopular with local residents at the time, but allowed the park to escape creeping urbanisation and become the oasis of green within the urban sprawl that it is today. It covers some 2,500 acres and is the home to around 630 deer. In 1906 an ill-fated attempt was also made to introduce roe deer to the park but the animals, brought in from Dorset, died out soon after release.

Today, the largest variety of captive deer can probably be found in Berlin, where a recent list numbered no less than 11 species and sub-species kept in the Zoo and a further 16 in the Tierpark.

The deer park at Woburn Abbey in Bedfordshire was established in the mid-1600s with herds of red and fallow deer. When Herbrand Russell inherited the title of 11th Duke of Bedford in 1893, however, things changed, as he was an enthusiastic zoologist and collector as well as President of the Zoological Society of London. By the early twentieth century, Woburn was considered to hold the largest captive collection of deer in the world, reaching a peak of 42 species. Today it is still home to around 1,200 deer covering 9 species, including

the only herd of Rusa deer (an Indonesian species) to be found in the UK. It also has large numbers of Père David's deer, or milu, which the 11th Duke preserved as a species after they became extinct in their native China and the only breeding herd in the world existed at the time at Woburn. The red deer of the park are world-renowned for the quality of their antlers.

Musk is a waxy secretion produced by a gland in the genital area of the male musk deer of eastern Asia. It is used in Oriental medicine and the perfume industry and is the most valuable deer product known; prices of up to US$45,000 per kilogram have been paid for it. The male musk deer will produce little more than 25 grams in his lifetime, and fortunately the perfume trade has moved away from it towards cheaper synthetic alternatives. Although it can be taken from a live animal, and musk deer farms have been established for this very purpose mainly in Russia and China, illegal and unsustainable hunting is still considered to be a major threat to the species.

Velvet, the furry covering that protects the growing antler, has been used in Oriental medicine for centuries to treat conditions including arthritis, stomach ulcers, high blood pressure, penile dysfunction in men and infertility in women. It is also said to sharpen the brain, restore energy and promote the appetite and is claimed to be a powerful aphrodisiac. Whilst medical opinion varies regarding just how effective velvet actually is, the market for it in the East is so great that deer farms in New Zealand started to export it during the 1970s, achieving as much as NZ$250 (about £150) per kilogram at one point. Removing velvet from sensitive growing antlers full of blood vessels and nerves is, of course, not without controversy. Collection under anaesthetic is a legal requirement in New Zealand, but sadly not in some other countries where the practice is followed.

Thread made from the sinews of reindeer is considered to be ideal for repairing boots or sewing canoes made of hide. Once wet it swells, creating watertight seams.

Oriental medicine values a wide variety of what Westerners would consider useless deer by-products: these include tails, blood, testes and penises. Dried deer foetuses are also much sought-after in some parts of Asia, and 'three-pizzle wine' is said to cure memory loss, anaemia and shingles.

According to the 1486 *Book of St Albans*, attributed to Dame Juliana Barnes, a list of 'proper' collective terms includes the information that a group of deer is referred to as a *herd* or a *mob*, while a group of foresters is a *stalk*. A group of roe, delightfully, shares the same term as a group of ladies – a *bevy*. My absolute favourite, though, has nothing to do with deer at all: it is a *flourish of strumpets*.

Whilst the British talk about deer stalking, elsewhere in the world it is more usually referred to as hunting. On the Scottish hill, however, the term 'stalker' is usually reserved for the professional who guides the person who is going to take the shot into position. The latter is more properly known as the 'rifle' or (and perhaps rather less PC) the 'gentleman'.

The stalker can also be referred to as the gillie or ghillie, a word which has its origins in the Gaelic word meaning an attendant on a Highland chieftain. In Robert Louis Stevenson's Kidnapped *there is reference to a character's father who 'was in the Black Watch, when first it was mustered; and, like other gentlemen privates, had a gillie at his back to carry his firelock for him on the march'.*

A largely obsolete term for a two-year-old roe buck is *gazelle*, and a roe doe of the same age a *girl*.

The Last Bite, or Der Letzte Bissen, *is a hunting custom in many European countries whereby a sprig of vegetation is placed in the mouth of a slain deer or other animal to see it into the next world*

There are many variations on the legend of Herne the Hunter. One tells that he was a keeper in Windsor Forest at the time of King Richard II who hanged himself after incurring the king's displeasure. Since then Herne has been said to haunt the forest. Shakespeare wrote in *The Merry Wives of Windsor*:

> *There is an old tale goes, that Herne the hunter,*
> *Sometime a keeper here in Windsor forest,*
> *Doth all the winter time at still midnight,*
> *Walk around about an oak, with great ragg'd horns;*
> *And there he blasts the tree, and takes the cattle;*
> *And makes milch-kine yield blood, and shakes a chain*
> *In a most hideous and dreadful manner*

The tree that Herne is reputed to have hanged himself from, Herne's Oak, was blown down in 1863 at which time it was estimated to be 700 years old.

The Peruvian tree deer Cervus arborealis *is the only deer species known to regularly climb trees. They do this to reach the nutritious buds, fruit and new leaf growth in the lower forest canopy. A small, lightly built deer about the size of a roe, they have simple antlers with a backwards curve, which have evolved to avoid hooking into the dense foliage. As a unique adaptation among deer, they have hooked cleaves on the forefeet along with highly developed dew claws, which enable them to scale trunks to reach heights of up to fifty feet off the ground where their lightly dappled brown and black coat helps to conceal them from their main predators, the jaguar, the vicuña, and the Andean condor.*

Santa's reindeer were first named in *A Visit from St Nicholas*, a poem written by Clement Clark Moore and first published in 1823. It later became better known as *The Night Before Christmas*. The eight reindeer pulling Santa's sled – Dasher, Dancer, Prancer, Vixen, Comet, Cupid, Donder (later renamed 'Donner') and Blitzen – were not joined by their more famous companion until the 1939 poem *Rudolph the Red-Nosed Reindeer* by Robert L. May.

Police in Illinois were surprised to receive a telephone call from Father Christmas to report that one of his reindeer was missing. It turned out not to be a hoax – the animal, called Mistletoe, had jumped out of its trailer on the way to a children's party. It was found safe and well after a police search.

In 1996, an over-zealous traffic policeman issued parking tickets to a milk float being pulled by eight reindeer at a Christmas event in Manchester. Their regular sleigh had to be hidden from sight to escape a similar fate. The owners of the animals, from the Reindeer Centre at Aviemore, were quoted as saying that 'Dancer and Prancer and their colleagues were too angry to comment'.

Every year without fail, one major broadsheet newspaper carries pictures of the red and fallow deer rutting in Richmond Park. The photographs themselves are stunning, but spoilt somewhat by inaccurate captions which almost invariably refer to red 'bucks' and fallow 'stags'. Not so long ago the same paper surpassed itself with a weighty report about the future genetic integrity of our wild red deer. There were, it reported, grave concerns that they were hybridising with a non-native species – the muntjac. Despite wonderful images of satyr-like muntjac bucks roaming the countryside equipped with stepladders, the reporter might have more accurately identified the sika as the real culprit.

The garron, sometimes called a girn or a shelt, is a small, sturdy breed of Highland pony, traditionally used to transport red deer carcases off the hill after a successful stalk. Horses are naturally alarmed by the smell of blood so a good one can take years to train fully, and a specialist deer-carrying saddle can cost well over £2,000. Although a garron can get to places a wheeled vehicle cannot, they have a limited deer-carrying capacity and need a full-time handler. For such reasons mechanical alternatives have taken over in many places although some Highland estates do still use them.

The use of a stalking horse is an old practice whereby hunters would walk behind a trained and steady horse to hide them while they approached to within range of their quarry. The wild animals, viewing the horse as

non-threatening, would not be alarmed as they would be by the sight of a human. Today, the term 'stalking horse' commonly refers to similar deception tactics employed in finance or politics when a relatively innocuous third party is used to hide the identity of the real protagonist who can come forward only if their bid is successful, or drop back with their reputation untainted if it is not.

It is very likely the bayonet, a blade attached to the end of a musket or rifle, was not actually first used by the military but by hunters. Once discharged, a muzzle loading firearm took a long time to reload and was useless when faced with a wounded and aggressive quarry such as a wild boar. A dagger with a handle designed to plug into the end of the barrel would transform the musket into a pike for self-protection. The bayonet takes its name from the Basque town of Bayonne, which was a famous centre for cutlery making. The first reference to a 'bayonne dagger' appeared in the late sixteenth century, and the first recorded use of the bayonet by the British Army was at the Battle of Killiecrankie in 1689.

Because early firearms were not capable of the same levels of accuracy that we enjoy today, it was once normal practice for Highland stalkers to be accompanied by a deerhound. Some varieties stood as much as three feet high at the shoulder and weighed 100 pounds; their job was to follow up the shot and pull down a wounded animal for despatch by the stalker.

The Muckle Hart of Benmore was a large stag that was pursued continuously for six days and five nights by Charles St John in 1833. One night was spent in an illegal whisky bothy, which left his companions insensible. The hunt ended in a desperate struggle between St John and the stag, in the course of which St John lost his rifle. When he eventually recovered it he found that his remaining ammunition was too big for the bore, so he had to scrape one ball down to fit before he could reload and take the final fatal shot.

Although they have never really been substantiated, rumours persist that in about 1584 the young William Shakespeare was caught poaching deer on

Sir Thomas Lucy's land at Charlecote Park, some four miles from Shakespeare's home in Stratford-on-Avon, for which he was subsequently beaten and imprisoned. Several later accounts of his life written in the seventeenth century make the claim, although there are no known contemporary records to support it. As no details of Shakespeare's life exist for this period the truth may never be known, and many historians discount the story.

The Norman conquerors of England in 1066 quickly designated large areas of the country as royal forests, hunting preserves for the nobility where commoners were not allowed to hunt. The penalties for poaching were severe, and could involve death or blinding.

In Europe the penalties for poaching were just as savage, with branding or cutting off a hand as commonplace punishments for a first offence. Persistent offenders were hanged or decapitated. In one account from 1537, the Archbishop of Salzburg ordered that a peasant, who, having despaired of a stag raiding his crops and killed it, should be sewn up in the deer's skin and torn apart by the Archbishop's hunting hounds in the town market square.

Contrary to the stories of Robin Hood, a bow was not the preferred tool of the medieval deer poacher, being too obvious, difficult to conceal, and the danger of a wounded deer escaping with incriminating evidence in the form of the arrow. The poacher's real mainstays were traps, snares, sharpened stakes and slings. The latter were deadly in skilled hands and there is evidence that they were used to bring down quarry as large as red stags.

A popular video game of the late 1990s was *Deer Avenger*, a parody of big game hunting titles. In it the player controlled a cartoon deer called 'Bambo' who hunted a variety of human redneck caricatures using weapons ranging from catapults loaded with deer droppings to machine guns. To lure his targets in, a number of decoy calls could be employed; they included 'Does anyone want a beer?' and a seductive female voice which declared 'I'm naked *and* I've got a pizza'.

It is said that the use of the slang term 'buck', meaning a US dollar, has its origins in trading between early settlers and native American Indians. Deerskins had a stable value and were treated as units of currency in their own right, and so were used as a benchmark for the value of other items. One early frontier traveller recorded in his 1748 journal that a cask of whisky was worth five bucks, and elsewhere that someone had been robbed of the value of thirty bucks, referring presumably to skins and not cash. The expression 'to pass the buck' probably dates from over a hundred years later, when poker players would mark the dealer in a game by placing a buckhorn handled knife in front of him. When it was time for another player to take responsibility for dealing, the buck would be passed. US President Harry S Truman famously kept a sign on his desk declaring that 'The buck stops here'.

In 1854 the *Societé Zoologique d'Acclimatation* was founded in Paris, the first of many acclimatisation societies set up to encourage the introduction of non-native fauna and flora around the world. Many mistakes were made, resulting in some devastating environmental effects. The reasons for wanting to do this varied. Some European settlers in colonies around the world missed familiar animals from their home countries, while others wanted to 'improve' the local wildlife or to hunt for sport. Whatever the motivation, in this way deer made their way to many countries where they did not occur naturally. New Zealand alone gained seven deer species which still flourish there today, while others (such as the moose) failed to establish successfully. The new arrivals, in a country where the only naturally occurring mammals were bats, had an overwhelming impact on the available vegetation and the native species which depended on it, resulting in the New Zealand government eventually employing full-time cullers to reduce numbers. It was not until the 1980s that deer numbers were felt to be under any real control.

Between 1959 and 1960 nine Axis deer, native to India, were released on the Hawaiian island of Maui. Fifty years later the population was estimated

at 12,000 and doubling in size every four years. Environmentalists are now deeply concerned by increasing land erosion and the associated sedimentation which damages coral reefs. The annual economic damage caused by the deer is estimated in millions of dollars and hunters are now encouraged to pursue them without seasons or bag limits to try to contain the problem.

St Matthew Island, a remote area of about 128 square miles located off the coast of Alaska, was the scene of the release of 29 reindeer by the US Coastguard, as a food source and for recreational hunting, in 1944. When the coastguard station there was abandoned soon afterwards, the reindeer population exploded thanks to a lack of predators, and by 1963 had reached 6,000 animals. Then the lichen that the reindeer depended on for food ran out and over the course of a single winter there was a massive die-off. When researchers reached St Matthew Island in 1966 they found that only 42 animals, all but one of them cows, were still alive. The single bull remaining was infertile. Unable to reproduce, the reindeer population on the island had disappeared by the 1980s. The story of St Matthew Island is frequently held up as a classic case study of overpopulation and unsustainability.

The town of Douglas, Wyoming, issues tags permitting the hunting of the jackalope, a mythical creature with the body of a jackrabbit and the horns of a deer. The hunting season is short, being between sunrise and sunset on the 31st June, and it has been suggested that the hunter should not have an IQ higher than 72. The licensee must sign a declaration stating: 'I am a person of strict temperance and absolute trustfulness. I do reserve the right, at my discretion and if interrogated concerning my hunting experience, to employ such lingual evasion, loud rebuttal and double talk as the occasion and circumstances require.'

Taxidermists sometimes create composite creatures from parts of different mammals and birds. One such is the *wolpertinger* of Bavarian folklore that lives in the Alpine forests. It varies in form but usually has the antlers of a deer, head of a rabbit, body of a squirrel and wings of a bird.

Queen Elizabeth I greatly enjoyed shooting deer with a crossbow and was reputed to have been a very accurate shot. The form of shooting was hardly sporting, though: park deer would be driven past her in an enclosed area where she would be stationed inside a comfortable hide.

In parts of Scandinavia, hunting with an elk hound is a popular form of both sport and obtaining meat. One method involves training the hound to hunt loose and only start barking when it has finally brought the elk to bay. The hunter must then approach the stationary elk, without alerting it to his presence in which case it will move off again, and take the shot. Modern telemetry is often used to assist the hunter in tracking the position of his hound.

Before the development of modern firearms, red deer were often herded into enclosures on the Scottish hill to be killed with spears or other simple weapons. Later on, hunts involved driving the deer towards hidden marksmen. It was only during the Victorian era that stalking deer as we know it today became a fashionable activity in Britain. Although much of the popularity of Highland deer stalking has been attributed to Prince Albert, who introduced Continental practices to this country, the first recorded instance of a deer being stalked in the 'classic' style by a gentleman was by Cluny Macpherson, Chief of Clan Macpherson, in 1745. For a long time, obtaining meat for the table was left to servants, being considered an undignified activity for the privileged.

In 1885 a certain Colonel Fosbury invented a gun with rifling at the choked end of an otherwise smoothbore barrel, enabling it to be used as both shotgun and rifle depending on the ammunition employed. The patent was obtained by London gunmakers Holland & Holland, who marketed it as the Paradox gun (a paradox being a statement that apparently contradicts itself), as it was neither a true rifle nor shotgun.

The Paradox was made in a variety of sizes ranging from 8 to 20 bore, and was especially popular among sportsman travelling overseas who wished to reduce the weight of their baggage by taking only one gun. It also greatly improved shooting opportunities as ammunition could be chosen to suit the quarry that presented itself during an expedition. The gun was an immediate success, producing even patterns of shot as well as surprising levels of accuracy with heavy bullets at longer ranges.

The Girandoni air rifle, designed around 1779, was certainly no toy and actually saw service with the Austrian Army until about 1815, although there are no records suggesting that it was ever used in action. It was one of the earliest repeating rifles, firing up to thirty .46 calibre balls on a single charge of the cast iron air reservoir which also served as the butt. One was also carried on Lewis and Clark's expedition to explore and map what is now the western portion of the USA between 1804 and 1806, where it was used both for hunting and to impress the native tribes that were encountered. Despite the advantages of low noise, no smoke and a high rate of fire it never really caught the imagination in other countries. The reservoir took 1,500 strokes on a hand pump to charge and the mechanism was very delicate, while manufacturing was slow and costly using the technologies available at the time. Modern reproductions have produced muzzle energies of between 150 and 200 foot pounds and are claimed to penetrate a pine plank one inch thick at a distance of one hundred yards.

During the 1950s deer stalkers were just beginning to employ telescopic sights; hitherto the use of open sights was commonplace. Gunmaker and sportsman David Lloyd, who is credited with grassing 5,000 red deer stags during a stalking career lasting sixty years, was impatient of the inadequate mounts then available for attaching telescopic sights to sporting rifles. He designed and launched a revolutionary rifle design in which the scope was integral to the rifle itself. It was initially available in .244 Holland & Holland Magnum (Lloyd's own development), .264 Winchester Magnum and .25-06 Remington, all of which are powerful cartridges with flat trajectories producing good terminal energy at longer ranges. Lloyd's intention was to create a rifle that would maintain its zero despite rough use and heavy recoil, and many customers reported that they never had to adjust their sights despite years of regular use. The Lloyd rifle has a distinctively streamlined appearance and is widely sought by collectors today, although modern mounting systems have largely overcome the problems experienced by stalkers some sixty years ago.

A remarkable flintlock firearm, mounted on a tripod and with rotating cylinders similar to those found on a modern revolver, was patented by London lawyer James Puckle in 1718. Way ahead of its time, it was complicated and never achieved popularity. One curious aspect of its design was that it could be fitted with two different cylinders, one of which fired rounded projectiles while the other employed square bullets designated on the patent for use against Turks, to 'teach them the benefits of Christian civilisation'.

A combination gun has long been a popular form of firearm on the Continent, where it is used for driven hunts or battues. Consisting of a rifled barrel mounted next to one or more smoothbore barrels, it allows the hunter to choose shot or bullet as appropriate to the furred or feathered target that presents itself. The most common set-up is two shotgun barrels mounted above a rifle, but variants can include over-and-under, triple barrel shotgun/ fullbore/smallbore combinations, or as many as four barrels in total. A gun with three barrels is known as a drilling (from the German *drei*, meaning three), while a vierling has four barrels.

There are an estimated 60,000 collisions involving deer and motor vehicles every year in England alone. The peak times for accidents tend to be between 6pm and midnight, and then 6am and 9am, the morning rush hour. About 40 percent of these involve fallow, followed by 32 percent roe and 25 percent muntjac. In Scotland the picture is different, reflecting different deer population structures, where 69 percent of casualties are roe and 25 percent red deer.

American deer species continue to crop up in unexpected places, probably thanks to the over-reliance of design artists on transatlantic image libraries.

In 2013, signs in Richmond Park advising visitors not to disturb the deer and to keep dogs on leads featured a picture of a white-tailed buck, a species certainly not present there. In the same year, the Scottish National Heritage logo for their 'Scotland's Big 5' campaign promoting wildlife tourism also included the silhouette of a white-tailed buck instead of a red stag as was presumably intended.

In the 1938 film Adventures of Robin Hood, *Errol Flynn enters a feasting hall with a deer carcase, supposedly killed in Sherwood Forest, on his shoulders. It's a mule deer, though, and these are only found on the western side of the USA.*

The invention of the hot air balloon by French paper-makers Joseph-Michel and Jacques-Étienne Montgolfier in the late 1700s quickly caught society's imagination, and a number of showmen went to extreme lengths to try to outdo each other. In 1817, lifting off from the Tivoli Gardens of Paris, a Monsieur Margat made a balloon ascent seated on his pet stag Coco, described as a *cerf aéronaute*. A contemporary engraving shows Margat dressed in the uniform of a dragoon, with Coco fully tacked up with reins, saddle and stirrups. An onlooker recorded: 'On making the ascent, the deer did not show any anxiety; it cast its eye upon the brilliant company and seemed to take great pleasure in the repeated applause of the spectators. The change to a very great height seemed to concern it. The formation of a storm mixed with lightning decided the aeronaut to make his descent on the level field called Des Bruyères three quarters of a league away, where, still mounted upon his deer, he was led in triumph by the inhabitants to the mayor, who accorded him the best of receptions.'

In 2005 the owner of a game ranch in Texas introduced the concept of 'Internet hunting', whereby a remotely controlled rifle could be aimed by computer to shoot a variety of live game animals. Its inventor justified this as allowing disabled people the chance to enjoy 'an authentic hunting experience'. The practice was immediately condemned by most hunting and animal welfare organisations and by 2008 was banned in forty US states, mostly as a preventative measure. There is no evidence that it takes place today.

Britain is one of the few countries in the world where it is possible to hunt deer all year round (according to species and sex), and where there are no bag limits. Contrast this with the USA where hunting seasons are short; they vary from state to state and may be altered annually, sometimes lasting only a few weeks. Archers and those with muzzle loaders are allowed extended dates, which has made these methods increasingly popular. Tag limits are usually strictly enforced.

It is notoriously difficult to count wild deer. In the early 1960s, as part of a research programme, it was decided to remove the roe deer population, estimated at around 70 animals, from about 200 hectares of woodland at Kalø, Denmark. By the end of the cull, 213 roe had actually been shot.

Research in Denmark has indicated that a simple instance of roe deer disturbance by human activity, such as dog-walking, demands that the deer may need to eat an extra 310 grams of food to replace the energy expended. Longer term disturbance, involving extended or repeated occasions of flight, might require as much as an extra 2.7 kilograms. In calorific terms this translates as .2 kilocalories if the deer is slightly disturbed by a passing bicycle, 9kcal if chased by a dog, or a massive 76.5kcal if continually moved on by a six hour orienteering event.

The death toll from hunting accidents has been reduced in the USA from a massive 1,500 fatalities a year in the 1960s to around 400 a year today. This is thanks largely to extensive hunter safety education programmes. Almost three out of four accidents are self-inflicted, and caused by factors ranging from falling off cliffs to negligent firearms handling. In instances where one hunter has been shot by another, in many cases the victim was mistaken for a game animal, or the shooter fired blindly into cover.

Unsurprisingly, estimates show that the USA has the highest incidence of gun ownership in the world, with some 97 privately owned firearms in circulation for every 100 residents. It is followed by Serbia with 58. Northern Ireland has 21.9, while England and Wales, and Scotland are much further down the list with 6.2 and 5.5 respectively.

In 2013 a Norwegian hunter shot at a moose, missing it but hitting a man sitting on the lavatory in a hut behind it. The man was struck in the abdomen and airlifted to hospital where he later recovered; the moose escaped unharmed and the hunter was arrested.

Taxidermy, so popular among the Victorians, has enjoyed a resurgence in fashion in recent years and it is quite usual to see mounted heads featuring in modern home design features in magazines and the Sunday newspaper supplements. Although man has been treating skins so that they can be used as clothing and shelter for thousands of years, the practice of stuffing them with horsehair or rags to produce a supposedly lifelike representation of the animal only started in the early nineteenth century. The work was originally done by furniture upholsterers. Some efforts ranged from the puzzling to the truly frightening. The modern taxidermist is more likely to use a sculpted 'form' of modern material onto which the skin is mounted, and the finished product can be a work of art in its own right.

The word 'taxidermy' is taken from the Greek taxis, *meaning arrangement, and* derma *meaning skin. It has no connection with a taxi cab, which has its roots in the Latin* taxa, *to charge.*

If you shoot a special animal which you would like to preserve as a shoulder mount, don't forget to cut up the *back* of the neck (rather than the usual gralloching cut up the front) and skin back as far behind the shoulders as you can to give the taxidermist plenty of material to work with. Sever the head at the axis joint just behind the skull and don't try to skin it yourself as this involves very delicate work – leave that to the expert.

All material destined for the taxidermist needs to be delivered as quickly as possible as otherwise the hair may start to 'slip' or fall out. Alternatively, the head and skin can be deep frozen as a temporary measure to preserve it (although it would make sense to warn other freezer users first).

Sadly, the quality of taxidermy can vary between practitioners and I have seen some deer heads which looked more like badly stuffed teddy bears. If you come across a taxidermist whose work you like, it is always worth collecting a business card or at least making a note of contact details against the day that you shoot an animal that you would like to have mounted.

If, when boiling out a skinned trophy head, the nasal bones become separated from the main part of the skull there is no need to panic. Once dry they will slot neatly back into place and can be fixed with PVA wood glue. The latter dries clear and creates a strong bond with bone. It's also very useful for emergency repair work if a trophy is damaged and needs to be reassembled.

If you have a dog in the household, do take care not to leave trophies lying about within their reach. My own prized first roebuck skull had to be cut down radically after it was stolen from a coffee table by the pointer puppy we owned at the time and which greatly enjoyed gnawing down the nose end.

I know of a couple, both keen hunters, who have 'his and her' mounted warthog heads on either side of the marital bed. To my knowledge they have never had children.

The walls and ceiling of the ballroom at Mar Lodge, near Braemar, are decorated with the antlers of some 2,200 stags dating back to the Victorian era. Although probably not to everyone's taste, it is still a very popular venue for weddings and other functions.

Emperor Franz Joseph I of Austria (1830–1916) was a keen hunter who is credited with shooting some 55,000 game animals, including deer and chamois, during the course of his life. His preferred summer retreat was his hunting lodge near Bad Ischl where he liked to dress and live simply (one of his favourite meals was boiled beef and beer) and spend as much time as possible hunting. The imperial lodge at Ischl has been maintained very much as it would have appeared in Franz Joseph's day and is decorated extensively with the Emperor's sporting trophies. It remains in family hands but is open for tourists to visit.

White stags crop up frequently in mythology. In Arthurian legend the uncatchable white stag represents man's continual quest for knowledge; the idea is reflected in The Chronicles of Narnia *where the White Stag is reputed to grant wishes to whoever catches him. Killing a white deer of any kind was considered to be very unlucky, and in Celtic mythology white deer were considered to be other-worldly messengers that would change the lives – for good or bad – of those who encountered them.*

King David I of Scotland was said to have gone hunting on the Feast Day of Holy Rood against his priest's advice in 1128. In pursuit of a white stag, he was thrown from his horse when the deer turned on him. Grasping its antlers to protect himself, he prayed to God to save him whereupon the antlers turned into a cross and the beast vanished. King David was inspired to build a shrine to the miracle at the spot where it occurred – Holyrood Abbey. ('Rood' is an ecclesiastical term for a cross or crucifix.)

King James VI of Scotland apparently became obsessed by a white stag that he spotted while hunting near Braemar in 1622. He summoned the Royal Forester, John Scandaver, and instructed him to catch the beast so that it could be taken to the royal deer park at Windsor. After Scandaver's early attempts failed, a grander plan using some 700 beaters to drive the animal into a trap was employed but also came to nothing. It was only the king's death in 1625 that brought such efforts to a halt, and the stag remained at liberty.

The open seasons for shooting deer in England and Wales can be a little confusing, but there is an easy way to remember them.

- Start with **roe bucks** – you can shoot them from April Fool's Day until they come back to haunt you at Hallowe'en: **1 April – 31 October**
- When you are not shooting roe bucks, you can shoot **all female deer** and **Chinese water deer bucks: 1 November – 31 March**
- **Large male deer (red, sika and fallow)** are only safe for three months in the summer, May, June and July, and can be shot from <u>A to A</u>: **1 August – 30 April**

There is of course no close season for muntjac of either sex.

The wild boar, absent from Britain for centuries, is now re-established in several places thanks largely to escapees from farms and rumoured deliberate releases. Anecdotal evidence suggests that they have been spotted in a wide number of counties, although the main populations seem to be centred on Gloucestershire, Dorset and East Sussex. Some reports, though, need to be taken with a pinch of salt as muntjac, with their hunched, pig-like appearance, are occasionally mistaken for boar by people who are not used to seeing them.

In the Forest of Dean the boar population, thought to have been introduced illegally in 2004, might now number over 600 and is reported to be doubling in size every year. Despite increasing incursions by boar onto farmland and into household gardens, where they plough up crops and gardens, raid rubbish bags, frighten horses and are increasingly involved in traffic accidents, there is still resistance to culling by some.

There is no set season or minimum firearm calibre for shooting wild boar in Britain although they fall under the more general protection offered by laws such as the Wildlife and Countryside Act 1991 and the Wild Mammals Protection Act 1996. As a large and potentially dangerous animal, it has been

suggested that a .270 calibre rifle with appropriate ammunition should be considered an absolute minimum, and that great care should be taken not to shoot sows with dependent young. Shooters should also ensure that the conditions on their Firearms Certificate actually allow them to use the rifle for boar.

Wild boar probably became extinct in Britain by the thirteenth century. There have been many unsuccessful attempts to reintroduce them since, mainly by private landowners for hunting. James I had them released into Windsor Park in the early seventeenth century, and his son Charles I also oversaw their introduction to the New Forest. The boar did not prosper though, no doubt because locals were not prepared to tolerate the destruction they caused to crops. Today's free-living population probably owes much of its success to the growth in popularity of boar farming since the 1970s.

In 2014, more than one in three wild boar shot by hunters in Saxony were found to carry excessive levels of radiation, rendering them unfit for human consumption. This is probably a legacy of the 1986 Chernobyl nuclear disaster; although over 700 miles away, radioactive particles were released into the atmosphere before falling and contaminating the soil. Boar are considered especially susceptible as their diet contains large amounts of truffles and other fungi which store radiation. Tests have been compulsory since 2012, and carcases exceeding the safe limit of more than 600 becquerels per kilogram are destroyed.

The inaugural meeting of the British Deer Society took place at Woburn on the 24th February 1963. The BDS started as a special interest group of the largely academic Mammal Society but broke away to pursue political lobbying in the interests of deer welfare. It was strongly influential in the final forms of the Deer (Scotland) Act of 1959 and the Deer Act 1963. Today the promotion of deer welfare, through education, research and lobbying, remains the Society's principal aim.

The winter of 1962-63, which lasted from Christmas until early March, brought extended periods of sub-zero temperatures, blizzards and deep snow. It was one of the coldest winters on record and had a catastrophic effect on British wildlife. Food was difficult to find and almost every water source was frozen solid. The bird population was reduced by half and populations of some species, such as the wren, declined by as much as 80 percent. Records were not kept for mortality among deer but carcases were widespread, including those discovered in outbuildings and garages where the animals had presumably sought shelter.

One informed observer suggested that mortality among muntjac in some places probably exceeded 70 percent. Only predatory species such as the fox did well with plentiful supplies of weakened prey and carrion to feed on.

The USA has some interesting state laws. In Alaska, it is illegal to push a live moose out of an aircraft in flight, while in Tennessee no game except whales may be shot from moving vehicles (Tennessee is a landlocked state). In Kansas, on the other hand, rabbits may not be shot from motor boats and you may not use a mule to hunt ducks. Texans are not permitted to shoot a buffalo from the second storey of a hotel, and in Florida sexual relations with a porcupine are forbidden. Reassuringly though, in Maryland a lion may not be taken into a cinema and in Massachusetts gorillas are not allowed on the back seat of any car. The most worrying thought, however, is just why creating these regulations was ever considered necessary in the first place.

In the opening credits of the blockbusting television series Game of Thrones, *the sigil of House Baratheon is represented on the shield portraying the houses of the four main protagonists as a white-tailed buck. Throughout the series, though, the only deer seen are reds, unsurprisingly as much of the series is filmed on location in Ireland. The Emmy Award-winning titles were created by a California-based company.*

Oliver Fisher Winchester, the founder of the firearms company bearing his name, originally manufactured men's shirts before producing the

Winchester rifle in 1866. The rifle, a repeater with a tubular magazine below the barrel, which became synonymous with the American West, was actually a development of an earlier design by Benjamin Henry.

It is believed that the word 'gun' is derived from the Norse female name Gunhildr, meaning war. Its first recorded use comes from a fourteenth century catapult listed among the weapons in the English Exchequer and described as Lady Gunhilda. Over time, the term became shortened to gonne and finally gun.

In April 1910 Theodore Roosevelt, having just completed his term as US President, set out on an epic expedition to east and central Africa to collect specimens for the Smithsonian Institution and the National Museum of Natural History, then under construction in New York. The party was led by professional guide RJ Cunninghame and joined occasionally by legendary hunter Frederick Selous, and cost the modern equivalent of about $2million. Less than a year later over 23,000 specimens ranging from insects to elephants had been collected, including over 5,000 mammals, 4,000 birds and 2,000 reptiles. Many of the 512 big game animals in the final tally were hunted by Roosevelt himself and it is said that it took over eight years to finally catalogue all of the collected material. The expedition also collected live animals, including lion, leopard, cheetah and antelope for the National Zoological Park.

How often have you had a deer, for no obvious reason, suddenly spook and disappear when all of the circumstances suggest that the stalker should not be detectable? Some hunters swear that deer, as well as other large game animals, have a 'sixth sense' that can detect the presence of predators. The idea is not new, and is common among many ancient hunting cultures. Some claim that the deer can pick up a person concentrating on them – one suggestion has been to count backwards from one hundred whilst stalking to reduce the effect of concentrating on your quarry, or not to stare too hard at the animal for more than a second or two at a time to reduce the 'predatory vibe'. Others suggest

that human bodies emit an electromagnetic signal that the animals can pick up; you can even buy suits which claim to reduce this. The fact remains that there is, of course, no real substitute for good fieldcraft when approaching a deer to get close enough to ensure that final, well-aimed shot.

Long before deer antlers were prized by hunters as trophies of the chase, they served a vital function as tools. Sections of antler would be used as hammers by early man who employed them to produce sharp flint tools, and numerous examples bearing strike marks have been found at archaeological sites both in Europe and the USA. They also served as digging implements; at the Neolithic flint mining complex at Grimes Graves, Norfolk, some 4,000 naturally shed red deer antlers have been recovered. These were used as picks, and scientists have determined that right-handed users preferred to use antlers from the left side of the deer's head.

The first examples of man's creativity most probably relate to hunting, being cave pictures dating back to the Palaeolithic era; some of the earliest examples may be as much as 30,000 years old. They have been found in caves around the world, some of the most famous being the Cantabria caves in Spain and the Lascaux caves in south-west France. Early hunters would celebrate the animals that they saw or killed by painting them on the walls of the caves using mineral pigments or engraving them. It has been variously suggested that the pictures were painted in honour of the animals killed, as accounts of successful hunts, or as pre-hunt rituals designed to bring good luck. The animals depicted at Lascaux include deer, aurochs (an extinct form of wild ox), horses, bison and big cats, all easily identifiable. One painting shows a man lying dead with a broken spear next to a bison which presumably had got the better of him. Many of the paintings are truly remarkable; an awestruck Pablo Picasso, after viewing the paintings at the Lascaux Cave, declared: 'We have learned nothing in twelve thousand years.'

'Texas heart shot' is a euphemistic term describing a shot taken at a fleeing animal, aimed at the base of the tail, and intended to either rake the spinal column, break a major bone and incapacitate the animal, or penetrate through the gut to the vital organs. The practice is frowned upon by responsible stalkers on both sides of the Atlantic. Quite apart from the welfare aspects of such a risky shot, and an inhumane one to boot, the carcase would almost inevitably be contaminated by stomach contents from the ruptured digestive tract. Just why it is attributed to Texas is unknown. That sage among American shooters, Jeff Cooper, summed up the practice in *The Art of the Rifle*: 'It's impolite, tends to wreck the carcass and doesn't bring the game down.'

In 1997 it was reported that a moose, apparently drunk on fermenting apples that it had eaten, was shot by a hunter near Stockholm after it had chased two boys. 'As I approached him he was tossing his head and I could tell by his eyes that he was out of it', the hunter said afterwards. 'When I cut him open a strong smell of fermenting fruit came from the stomach.'

Deer frequently feature on pub names and their signs. The most popular name by far is *The White Hart*, followed by *The Stag* and *The Roebuck*. Others include *Stag & Pheasant*, *Haunch of Venison* and *Stag's Head*. Some particularly innovative signs feature the same animal in summer coat on one side of a hanging board and winter coat on the other.

Despite being first produced almost 120 years ago, the Mauser Model 98 rifle action forms the basis of a large percentage of sporting firearms produced today. Designed originally for military use, it was quickly recognised as rugged, accurate and reliable, and has been shamelessly copied by a large number of other manufacturers. Peter Paul Mauser, its inventor, was born in 1838 and raised to the nobility by his native Germany in 1912 in recognition of his genius and dedication to small arms research and development. When he died in 1913 after catching a chill while testing a new rifle design, Count von Zeppelin paid his respects by sending one of his airships to drop a wreath on the monastery where Mauser's body lay in state.

In April 2000, a set of antlers from the long-extinct giant Irish elk *Megaloceros* was sold by London auctioneers Christie's for a record £47,000. The antlers were dated to 10,500 BC, spanned ten feet, and had originally been retrieved from an Irish peat bog.

A driver in Hertfordshire was surprised to arrive at work to find a live muntjac buck trapped in the bumper of his car. He had noticed a slight bump but thought that it was a stone and kept on going; it was only after he arrived at work some twenty-five miles further on that the uninvited passenger was spotted by a colleague. The fortunate deer was checked over by a vet and found to have only superficial cuts and bruises before being released back into the wild. The vet, unwittingly, had probably broken the law, as rehabilitated muntjac may normally only legally be released within one kilometre of the point of collection, and only then under licence.

In 1710, Squire Peter Legh bet Sir Roger Mason 500 guineas (an enormous wager worth well over £300,000 today) that his gamekeeper could drive 'twelve brace of stag' on foot from his estate, Lyme Park in Cheshire, to Windsor. The deer were to be added to the Royal herd as a gift to Queen Anne. The task fell to keeper Joseph Watson, who was told that failure to complete the 209-mile drive would cost him 'his life and fortune'. Not only did Watson succeed in this astonishing feat, but he went on to live a full life, eventually dying in 1753 aged 105 after drinking, according to local legend, a gallon of malt liquor a day.

Tales from Glen Garron

The Redeeming River

Hasty words can demand desperate remedies

For ten days now the Colonel had fished and caught precisely nothing. Every morning after breakfast he had gone to the most productive pool on the River Garron that flowed through the glen bearing its name, and worked his way down it thoroughly. There was nothing wrong with his casting, he had the utmost confidence in his choice of fly pattern, and without conceit he knew that he possessed the skills of an angler who, with the exception of a tedious interruption or two when his sovereign had demanded his presence elsewhere to deal with her enemies, had fished and taken salmon with astonishing regularity. He was no beginner, took his craft seriously, and furthermore had fished the Dell Pool of the Garron since he was a boy.

Water conditions were perfect and he knew that the fish should have been there; his neighbours both up- and down-stream were reporting regular success. The Garron, a spate river, had flushed through only the week previously, bringing fresh, silver prizes up from the estuary, mostly grilse; but yesterday an eighteen-pounder, still with sea lice clinging to it, had been taken not half a mile downstream with the very fly pattern he was using. Why, he wondered, could he not catch anything?

Willie Cameron knew the answer and it did not please him. He felt a particular responsibility for the situation as the blame rested firmly on the shoulders of young Ben, the son of a keeper friend whom he had taken on as a favour for a three-week work placement from college. There was nothing wrong with Ben himself. After a shaky start, when he quickly discovered, in terms of one syllable, that his preferred uniform of unzipped wellies, grubby T-shirt and hand-rolled fag were not acceptable to Willie's eyes, he had worked hard and shown a quick sense of humour. He was clearly intelligent and possessed endless stamina, which Willie had tested to the limit during long days on the hill where Ben had never once failed to keep up with the head stalker's gruelling pace. Willie had taken to him quickly and seen real promise for the future, maybe even as underkeeper to his son Archie when he eventually took over the reins at Glen Garron.

Admittedly the lad could be a wee bit accident-prone. There had been that unfortunate business with the eggs on Ben's first day of the placement, which had caused Shuna the cook to reveal the sharper side of her tongue ('Rare crabbit, she was, and lucky the boy can dodge, else she'd have fetched him a guid skelp' reported Archie, who had been listening in with glee), and the Lodge rose beds still needed serious attention after he mistook reverse for first gear in the estate Land Rover. Willie had been forgiving, though, as he liked the lad, but even he had become decidedly tetchy after an anxious, three-hour search after Ben had been instructed to 'follow the burn' down to a meeting place. Ben, unfamiliar with Highland terms, had take his line from the edge of last year's blackened heather patches rather than the stream and had become hopelessly confused in the unfamiliar landscape. He was eventually discovered, by the hastily assembled search party, two miles out onto the open hill.

No, today had been the last straw. Willie had discovered precisely why there were no fish to be caught in the Dell Pool when he found none other than Ben in it, diving and swimming like an otter, that morning before breakfast. Under questioning, Ben admitted that he had been doing this every day since he arrived in Glen Garron. Willie, with a mixture of exasperation, concern for the lad's safety, and sheer annoyance that his charge was responsible for ruining the laird's fishing, had exploded.

Willie's anger in full flow was impressive and the stuff of local legend. As the volume rose, so he lapsed into increasing levels of Gaelic which Ben may not have understood but was in no doubt as to the general meaning. 'Ye're nae a keeper, ye're a blithering liability, tha's whit ye are!' he snapped from the top of the steps to the estate office. He slammed the door behind him, leaving Ben shaken and speechless in the yard. The Colonel, watching from inside, had witnessed the whole outburst. 'In the name of goodness, Willie, was that really necessary?'

These rages, though rarely seen, had battered the confidence of far older and more self-assured men and Ben, only recently turned eighteen years old and despite an outgoing and robust personality for his age, proved more sensitive than he cared to admit. He was deeply affected. He confided to Archie Cameron over his lunchtime piece that day that perhaps gamekeeping was not for him. Archie's clumsy attempts to cheer him up – 'Ach, take nae notice, it's only Da' – had no effect and the lad lapsed into a robotic silence for the rest of the day, speaking only when he was spoken to and carrying out his tasks mechanically. The next day he was no better and it was clear to anyone who cared to look closely that his enthusiasm and spirit were broken.

Willie felt terrible. In his anger he'd gone too far and crushed the lad, he knew, and he desperately wanted to return him to his previous confident self. In an attempt to make amends he took Ben to flight a few pigeons as he knew that the lad loved his shooting, but the boy simply went through the motions and missed far more than he hit. An evening visit to Willie's special hill loch where the trout were numerous and eager to bite produced no excitement either, whilst a night in the Kelpie with Archie achieved nothing beyond an uncommunicative detachment, a seeming immunity to Amanda the barmaid's abundant charms, and a crushing hangover the next morning which left Ben even more dejected.

How he could restore Ben's confidence in the few days left of the work placement, Willie realised with a sinking feeling, was beyond him. In desperation he sought out an old friend and ally whom he trusted and admired. If anyone could help, he thought, this person could.

A recent fall of heavy rain had caused the Garron to rise dramatically. It was now on the drop, and Lady Mary announced that she intended to fish the Brae pool just above the Dell. No mean hand with a fly rod herself, she knew that this was a productive spot on a falling river, but it could be treacherous in a fast current. Acknowledging her husband's parting plea to take care, she set off alone for the river. Wading carefully into the rushing water at the head of the pool, with the water just short of the top of her waders, she started to cast.

Both Willie and Ben, taking a break from repairing a nearby fence, saw her fall. Lady Mary took a step forward whilst lifting her rod into a fresh cast, and suddenly there was a flurry of arms as she made a vain attempt to maintain her balance. The next moment she was down, a splashing figure swept swiftly towards the base of the pool where the water narrowed into a foaming rush through some wicked looking rocks.

The old keeper and his charge ran to the river's edge. 'I canna swim!' Willie lamented, but it was Ben who acted. Without hesitation he threw himself into the water and with a few powerful overarm strokes quickly reached the floundering figure. Struggling, he managed to draw her back towards the bank where Willie was waiting to help them both out of the shallows and onto dry land. They lay there for a moment gasping. 'Dear Ben, how can I possibly thank you?' Lady Mary finally asked. Ben, embarrassed, could mutter only a quiet 'no need, really' in reply.

Lady Mary recovered swiftly and characteristically took charge. 'Come to the Lodge and get dry,' she told the two of them. 'Willie, could you see if you can retrieve the rod? It's my favourite.' Willie did as he was bid, only to find that the last fouled cast had miraculously managed to attach the treble hook at the end of the line to a tussock of grass on the bankside. 'Whit a bliddy stroke of luck,' he remarked, as he rejoined the others and they made their way back across the field.

'Yes,' Lady Mary replied, with a sideways glance and a smile. 'What luck indeed!'

For his remaining days at Glen Garron Ben was fêted as the hero of the hour. His last night before returning south was marked by a celebration at the Kelpie Inn for the entire estate staff, with a blushing Ben as guest of honour. There he was presented with a full shooting suit in Glen Garron tweed, hastily produced yet a perfect fit, from the laird and his wife. From Willie came a beautiful, hand-made stalking knife, and Archie, somewhat slyly, handed over an engraved hip flask, which sloshed encouragingly. Amanda waited until last before emerging from behind the bar to give Ben a long, lingering and not particularly sisterly kiss, to the cheers of the assembled party. The lad was driven off to catch the night train by Willie and Archie, grinning like a Cheshire cat and promising to return.

'I thought that went rather well,' remarked the Colonel, over a nightcap back in the drawing room of the Lodge.

'It did, didn't it?' Lady Mary replied, as she stood, leaning against the mantelpiece. Idly her hand went to a gold disc on a faded ribbon half hidden behind a photograph frame. She did not need to examine the medal to know what was engraved upon it: one side held a female figure depicting Triumph, the other a simple laurel wreath. The picture showed three waving, smiling girls in swimming caps and costumes standing on a podium decorated with five interlocking rings.

Lady Mary smiled as she remembered. What a wonderful city Montreal was, and how exciting that summer of 1976 had been.

A
SALMAGUNDI
OF
DEER BIOLOGY

Deer occupy their own family, the *Cervidae*, which belongs to the order *Artiodactyla*, the even-toed ungulates, meaning that the third and fourth digits of their feet are the main weight-bearers. There are ten families in all among the artiodactyls, including the *Suidae* (pigs), *Bovidae* (cattle, sheep, antelopes, goats and others), *Giraffidae* (giraffes and okapis) and *Camelidae* (camels and llamas). Another order, the *Perissodactyla*, contains horses, rhinoceroses and tapirs. The name of this group means 'odd toed', meaning that the middle toe is the main weight-bearer.

It is considered that, genetically and taxonomically, there is more difference between red and roe deer than there is between cattle and sheep.

Deer are herbivores (plant eaters). Most species are classified as browsers, meaning that they feed selectively on buds, shoots and other vegetation growing off the ground, whilst others are primarily grazers whose main food intake is grasses and other ground herbage. Many combine both feeding strategies. A look at an individual animal's muzzle will give a clue as to its main feeding habits: a grazer generally has a much wider mouth, designed for the bulk intake of foodstuffs.

All deer are ruminants. They have four separate chambers to their stomachs and use the first, the rumen, to store hastily eaten foodstuffs which can be regurgitated later to be chewed thoroughly. This ensures that the full nutritional benefit can be extracted during digestion. Rumination is a clever adaptation practised by many prey animals which allows them to feed quickly in areas where predators may be a threat. They can then retire to a safer place and 'chew the cud' at leisure.

Deer have an excellent sense of smell and stalkers must always pay close attention to wind direction if they are not to give away their presence. Red deer on the open hill in Scotland have been known to pick up human scent at a distance of well over a mile.

Hearing is one of the most important senses to deer, especially as a means of recognising danger. They are able to move each ear independently, to focus on sounds from two different sources at the same time.

The smallest deer in the world is the pudu of South America: a big buck will weigh no more than about 9 kilograms. Smaller yet are the chevrotains or mouse-deer of Asia and Africa but these are not really true deer and belong to a different family.

According to the IUCN Red List of Endangered Species, the world's rarest deer is the Bawean deer Axis kuhlii, *which is only found on a small island off the north coast of Java. Already considered to be rare by the 1980s, in 2008 it was moved onto the Critically Endangered list when the wild population was considered to be no more than 250 mature animals. Thanks to increased protection, numbers are now thought to be stable and possibly increasing. There are over 300 additional animals in zoos and captive breeding programmes.*

The male deer is usually larger than the female, and in many species this aspect of sexual dimorphism is very pronounced. This trend is actually reversed in two species of muntjac, though. These are the Fea's and Black Muntjacs found in Thailand and China respectively, and it has been suggested that the smaller size of the male is an adaptation allowing greater agility when fighting.

Although it is impossible to count wild deer accurately, the Parliamentary Office of Science and Technology estimated in 2009 that there were more than 1,545,000 deer in the United Kingdom. This figure may be very conservative, but suggests that the most numerous species by far is the roe (over 800,000), followed by red, fallow and then muntjac. Chinese water deer were considered the least numerous with a population of less than 10,000.

Of Britain's deer, only the male Chinese water deer and muntjac have canine tusks in their upper jaws that are long enough to be visible on the living animal. The red and the sika, however, carry vestigial canine tusks, which are easily located inside the mouth. The roe is at a stage of its evolution where the canine tusk has all but disappeared but tiny ones are very occasionally found on bucks and, even more rarely, does. The fallow, our most evolved deer, has virtually lost them completely.

All mature deer carry at least 32 teeth, which consist of 6 upper and lower premolars, along with the same number of molars, and in addition 6 incisors and 2 canines on the lower jaw. Some species, such as the muntjac, Chinese water deer, sika and red, also have regular canines present in the upper jaw making a total of 34. Deer do not have any teeth at the front of the upper jaw. Instead they use a hard upper pad within the mouth to grip foliage when grazing or browsing. Plants fed on by deer tend to show a ragged tear rather than the clean cut made by the front teeth of animals such as rabbits or hares.

All mature male deer normally grow antlers with the exception of the Chinese water deer and the musk deer (which occupies its own separate family and is not considered to be a true deer in any case).

Many species of deer like to wallow, although some such as the roe and muntjac never do. Wallows are usually created in wet, muddy depressions in the ground which the animals can roll in, coating themselves in mud as a protection against biting insects, to cool down in hot weather and for what seems to be a pleasurable activity in its own right. Stags may also urinate in the wallow to enhance their scent.

Of all the deer species, the reindeer is the only one in which the female, or cow, habitually produces antlers. Bulls and cows have different cycles for shedding and regrowth. The bulls will start to cast their antlers shortly after the rut, which takes place in October, whilst the cows will retain theirs until they give birth in May or June. It is believed that this is to ensure that the cows can assert their dominance and feeding rights during the critical period of gestation.

Most species of deer change their coat twice a year; the winter coat, with its long, hollow guard hairs and woolly undercoat, has excellent insulating properties. Animals can stand for long periods with their backs covered in snow without any apparent discomfort and their body heat not melting the covering.

As deer hair floats well, it is very popular for tying floating trout fly patterns such as sedges, emergers and that chalk stream favourite during the mayfly hatch, the Gray Wulff.

The naked area of skin on the nose of a deer is known as the rhinarium. *It is frequently moistened with the tongue to improve scenting ability, and it has also been suggested that it is an important organ of touch. For most deer it covers the whole of the nose area and is completely bare, but that of the moose is very small indeed. The caribou or reindeer has no rhinarium at all; these deer have to spend much of their lives in sub-zero temperatures and their noses are entirely covered in fine hair.*

Opinion is divided regarding how many distinct species the deer family contains worldwide but the number is at least 47. Disagreements about the status of some sub-species mean that we cannot be certain of an exact number. The most confusion revolves around the muntjac, of which at least three new species have been recognised by science since 1994 and two more are under consideration. A small deer discovered in a poacher's snare in 2002 has since been identified as a Sumatran muntjac, hitherto considered extinct since 1930.

The Giant or large-antlered muntjac Muntiacus vuquangensis *was only recognised in 1994. As far as we know it is found only in the Ammanite mountain range of Vietnam, Cambodia and the Lao People's Democratic Republic, where numbers are threatened by over-hunting and loss of habitat. Due to the remoteness of its range, little is known about its habits, which are probably solitary and similar to those of other muntjacs. It is about twice the size of any other muntjac species and a large buck*

can weigh up to 50 kilograms, about the size of a fallow doe. Its scientific name is taken from the Vu Quang nature reserve in Vietnam where it was first discovered.

For many years it was believed that the muntjac in Britain was a hybrid of the Reeves', or Chinese, and Indian species. Chromosome counts have since proved conclusively that this is not so, and our animal is the Reeves'. Although the two species are capable of hybridising, the offspring are sterile and cannot reproduce further.

In simple terms, chromosomes, consisting of DNA and protein, are part of the cell of a living organism which determine what it is and the characteristics it inherits. Most deer have in the region of 70, but the Reeves' muntjac, like humans, possesses only 46 and the Indian muntjak has the incredibly low figure of 7 for male and 6 for female animals – the lowest recorded number for any known mammal.

Deer are one of the few mammals not to possess a gall bladder, a small sac usually located next to the liver which produces bile to assist in the digestion of lipids (forms of food fat).

Females of all true deer species have four teats, with the exception of the musk deer which has only two. The musk deer is considered by some not to be a true deer in any case, occupying its own family, the Moschidae. *All other deer belong to the family* Cervidae.

New-born deer of almost all species are covered by pale spots, producing a dappled effect; the only exceptions are the young of the moose, sambar, rusa deer and reindeer which have uniform coloured coats. The dappling makes a hidden fawn very difficult to see in the long grass or leaf litter where it will be left to lie motionless while its mother feeds. The spots fade quickly as the fawn develops and in most species have all but disappeared well within the two months following birth.

Reindeer are the only species of deer considered to have been fully domesticated by man, a process that started perhaps as long as 3,000 years ago in Scandinavia and Siberia. Today there are believed to be some 2.5 million domesticated reindeer spread across nine countries. Although it is widely known that the Sami people of Lapland depend heavily on them for food, skins and even transport, reindeer are an even more important resource to some of the peoples of Mongolia and Russia.

Deer species other than reindeer have on occasion been employed as beasts of burden; moose have been successfully trained to pull sleds or even be ridden in America, Sweden and Russia, and in eighteenth-century England the eccentric Earl of Orford was famous for driving a carriage pulled by four red stags.

Some strange objects have been found in the stomachs of dead deer. These include polythene bags, baler twine, fired cartridge cases and even condoms. In Richmond Park alone, the ingestion of litter is believed to be responsible for the deaths of around five deer every year.

One unpleasant parasite of deer is the warble fly. The adult fly lays its eggs on the legs of the deer and the larvae, once hatched, work their way up to the animal's back. Once there they burrow into the skin and continue to develop, looking rather like oversized maggots, until they eventually burrow out again and fall to the ground to metamorphose into the adult fly. Another is the nasal bot fly, which lays its eggs in the nasal passages of the deer. Affected animals can be seen shaking their heads and licking their noses to try to free themselves of the irritation. Warble infestation is fairly common in Scotland among red deer. Nasal bot fly is also found north of the border, affecting both roe and red deer, but is rare in England.

The 'bezoar' recommended by Professor Snape in the Harry Potter stories as an antidote to poison is not a figment of author J.K. Rowling's imagination – such things really do exist, though whether they actually have magical

properties is doubtful. Bezoars occasionally form in the stomachs of many animals, including deer, when an indigestible object becomes stuck inside the digestive tract and over time becomes coated with minerals until it becomes smooth and hard. In many ways bezoars are a sort of mammalian pearl, having parallels with what happens when a foreign object becomes trapped inside a mollusc. They were once also prized as 'madstones', and credited with many qualities ranging from bringing good luck to the owner to curing snake bites, epilepsy or rabies.

The Latin name of the pampas deer of South America, Ozotoceros bezoarticus, reflects the local belief in the prized medicinal qualities of such a stone; a hunted pampas deer would reputedly spit out the stone to distract the hunter and thus save its life.

Campylognathie, or bent-nosed syndrome, is a rare condition which occasionally affects mammals including deer. It results in the nose bones and jaw growing at a twisted angle; there is no scientific explanation for the condition but it may be genetic. Some observers suggest that it follows the same laws that dictate the direction that water swirls in when emptying down the plug-hole of a bath. In the northern hemisphere the bend supposedly tends towards the right, and in the southern towards the left. Sadly, the examination of some British deer skulls with a distinct bend to the left does not bear this theory out.

Polydactyly is a genetic mutation which results in the growth of extra digits at the end of a limb. In deer, it often appears as though the animal has produced a second hoof on the end of a leg and the phenomenon has been noted in a number of species.

Chinese water deer

It is quite usual for Chinese water deer does to rut in the same year that they are born and give birth on their first birthday – the only British deer to do so.

The Chinese water deer is potentially the most rapid breeder of Britain's deer species. Although an exceptionally large litter of seven young was recorded for a captive animal, between one and three is more usual.

The Chinese water deer was first introduced into this country in the late nineteenth century. It is believed that England now supports at least ten percent of the world population.

Chinese water deer are the only deer species in Britain that never produce antlers. Instead the bucks grow particularly large canine teeth, which can be as much as seven centimetres long. They use these for fighting with other bucks and for self-defence.

The British deer that ruts latest in the year is the Chinese water deer, which does so in November and December. Fawns are born in the following May or June.

In its native China, the semi-digested milk found in the rumen of unweaned Chinese water deer fawns is given to children as a traditional cure for indigestion.

ROE DEER

The closest living relative of the roe deer is the American white-tailed deer.

The roe deer rut is not, as is commonly supposed, driven by the buck but the doe, who will lead her chosen consort to a rutting ground of her choosing and mate only when she is ready.

Only the roe doe has an anal tush – a tuft of hair like an inverted shaving brush at the base of her

white caudal, or rump, patch. It is not a tail, serves no noticeable purpose, and no other deer possesses such a feature. It is a vital aid to distinguishing bucks from does whilst culling during the winter months when the bucks have just cast their antlers.

The roe deer, never native to Ireland, was introduced successfully to Lissandell in County Sligo in 1870 using Scottish stock and prospered, producing some exceptional heads. For a number of reasons, the main one being forestry damage, they were eventually killed off by the beginning of the twentieth century. They have not been seen there again since, although further reintroductions in the Republic of Ireland have been rumoured in recent years.

The fortunes of the roe deer in mainland Britain have fluctuated wildly over the years. Once widespread and numerous, their status changed in the mid-fourteenth century when they were no longer considered as a noble quarry for hunting and were reduced from 'beasts of the forest' to 'beasts of the warren'. This permitted widespread hunting by commoners and the species declined to the point that, by the eighteenth century, roe were considered to be extinct across most of Britain with the exception of a remnant population in the north.

It is only thanks to reintroductions from Scotland and the Continent, coupled with the replanting of previously cleared woodland, that they have been able to flourish and spread once again. There are probably more roe in Britain today than there have ever been.

Perruque heads, most usually associated with roe deer, form when an interruption to the supply of testosterone causes antlers to continue growing when the living bone should instead have stopped doing so and hardened off. The condition is usually associated with damage to the testes, and the result is a spongy mass which can eventually cover the eyes and become flyblown. The animal will then suffer a protracted and unpleasant death; it should be culled without delay if seen. The term perruque *is taken from the curly wig traditionally worn by judges.*

Of all Britain's deer, it is the roe which seems to produce the widest variety of abnormal antlers. This probably has much to do with the growth cycle that occurs during the winter months; the other species renew their antlers during the spring and summer. Winter disturbance by shoots and other seasonal activities is probably responsible for fleeing bucks damaging the soft growing tissue resulting in malformations to the final antler. Once cast the next year, regrowth will usually produce normal antlers unless there is permanent damage to the pedicle, the bony outcrop on top of the skull from which they grow.

In 2008, a 'unicorn' roe deer was born in captivity in Italy. The young buck had only one pedicle in the centre of its head, from which a single antler grew. Its twin brother had perfectly normal double antlers and scientists have attributed the anomaly to a genetic flaw. It has been suggested that similar animals gave rise to the myth of the unicorn.

A white roe buck spotted in Dumfries & Galloway in 2009 was the subject of a media circus when *The Sunday Times* reported that foreign hunters were involved in a bidding war for the right to shoot the animal. The matter was even raised in the Scottish Parliament before the owner of the land decided not to sell the right to stalk it after all. It was later reported as having rutted successfully, though there is no evidence that its unusual genes have actually been passed on.

MUNTJAC

Unlike our other deer species, muntjac breed all year round. There is no close season for them and they can be shot legally at any time. To avoid orphaning a dependent fawn, the shooting of only smaller does, and mature does which are heavily pregnant, is recommended. This will ensure that any previous offspring will be well grown and independent of their mothers. Thin, mature does have probably given birth recently and will have a dependent fawn hidden nearby. A mature doe closely pursued by a buck has likewise probably just given birth and come into season again. Bucks can be safely shot at any time of the year.

Mature muntjac bucks cast their antlers in May or June and regrow them by the end of August. Immature bucks carrying their first set of antlers have to wait until they can fall in line with the adult antler cycle, so a muntjac seen in velvet outside the summer months might be anything between under a year and two years old.

∞∞∞∞∞∞◇∞∞∞∞∞∞

In areas of high muntjac density, it is not unusual to find that many bucks have ripped ears and heavy scarring. This is mostly caused by fighting amongst themselves, using the sharp inner edge of their canine tusks as formidable weapons.

FALLOW

A fallow buck with his first set of antlers is commonly known as a pricket. Thereafter in successive years, according to the old formal language of hunting, he is referred to as a sorrel, sore buck, bare buck, buck and eventually a great buck.

∞∞∞∞∞∞◇∞∞∞∞∞∞

A disturbed fallow deer will bounce away with all four legs leaving the ground simultaneously. This is known as 'pronking' or 'stotting'. Some observers believe that this could be an alarm signal to others, or the deer's way of showing a

potential predator that it is fit, healthy and not worth pursuing. It is also done by some other deer and antelope.

In the Mortimer Forest, Shropshire, some fallow deer have distinct ear tufts and longer body hair than normal. This is the only place in the world where such fallow are found. The feature is considered to be caused by a dominant gene and can occur among all of the fallow colour varieties.

The arrival of the fallow deer in Britain was a major factor in establishing the popularity of deer parks. Initially fallow would have been rare and kept as a status symbol for display and admiration rather than a source of food or quarry for hunting. In the Domesday Book of 1086, 37 parks were recorded; by the year 1300 this number had grown to something in the region of 3,000.

Britain is not the only place where fallow deer have been introduced and flourished. Outside Europe they can be found as far afield as North and South America, Australia, New Zealand and the West Indies.

Fallow deer are the only British deer which have defined regular colour varieties: the familiar spotted common, the paler menil (which retains its paler colour in winter, unlike the common which grows a grey coat), black, and white. The single fawn, which is born in June or July, is not always of the same colour variety as its parents.

White fallow evoke mixed responses among deer stalkers. Quite apart from many people considering it to be bad luck to shoot a white animal, some managers prefer to leave them as 'markers', to give away the position of the better camouflaged animals with which they are herding. This is, of course, a double-edged sword and others prefer to remove them from the ground because they can attract the attentions of poachers.

SIKA

The first Japanese sika brought to Britain were a pair exhibited at Regent's Park Zoo in 1860. The first English feral population probably originated from Brownsea Island in Poole Harbour, Dorset, where a number of them were released in 1896 and promptly swum ashore, while they were deliberately released in Scotland and Ireland as early as the 1860s and 1870s. Further escapes from parks and deliberate releases have boosted their presence elsewhere ever since.

∞∞∞∞∞◇∞∞∞∞∞

During the rut, the sika stag will often produce milky 'tears' from the gland in front of each eye (the suborbital gland).

∞∞∞∞∞◇∞∞∞∞∞

Of all the deer species, sika have a particular reputation for ferocity. Wounded animals have been known to behave aggressively towards stalkers and dogs which approach them, and a second shot from a safe distance is recommended if there is any doubt about the animal's condition before approaching it.

RED

The upper canine tusk, or tush, of the red deer is greatly prized by some Continental stalkers for making jewellery items such as tiepins or brooches. They are also known as *grandeln*, and selling them to dealers used to be an important perk of the Highland estate stalker. Value was determined by size, colour and condition, and in the

1950s a good set could fetch as much as £5. Sadly, the market has all but disappeared today.

∞∞∞∞∞◊∞∞∞∞∞

In October 2010 there was a media frenzy concerning the killing of a Devon red stag, dubbed the 'Emperor of Exmoor' by a local photographer. There were varying claims that poachers or legitimate stalkers were responsible; others said that the stag was in fact still alive and well and that the story had been manufactured for a variety of reasons. Whatever the truth of the matter, it was the legal shooting season at the time. The stag was reported as weighing an estimated 136 kilograms and claimed by some to be the largest living wild deer in Britain, no doubt to boost the sensational aspect of the story. This is almost certainly untrue, as the red deer found in parts of East Anglia are acknowledged as some of the largest in the country and a good stag there can weigh as much as 180 kilograms.

Tales from Glen Garron

The Wrong Shades of Grey

Appropriate retribution from an unlucky thirteen

'Ach, whit a bliddy shame.'

Archie Cameron shook his head sadly. He had been checking for signs of deer in the new plantation when he came upon the small bundle of feathers lying motionless in the heather. Still warm, the bird had clearly flown into the six-foot fence that surrounded the vulnerable small trees and had broken its neck. Never one to waste anything, he tucked it into his haversack to feed to his ferrets later on and continued with his patrol.

* * * * *

A state of friendly rivalry existed between the estates of Glen Garron and neighbouring Inverpockle. The Colonel and Lord Pockle had been at school together and later served in the same regiment, while Willie Cameron and his opposite number, Duncan Mackenzie, were regular drinking companions in the Kelpie Inn. Today, though, the gloves were off for the annual clay shoot, which would be followed in the afternoon by a grouse drive, which traditionally took place at alternating estates each year.

This year it was the turn of Glen Garron to host the neighbouring laird and his staff, so Willie, assisted by the Colonel and his regular team, would run the beating line and hopefully provide some sport. The bags were never particularly large – fifteen brace to a team of eight guns was considered exceptional – but the day was always eagerly anticipated by both sides.

In any case, the clay shoot in the morning was considered to be the far more important event, as it would determine which team picked up the drinks bill at the Kelpie that evening. This was no small matter; the landlord knew from experience just how uninhibited free drinks could make the winners, and always laid in extra supplies of the very finest vintage malt for the occasion. Willie was confident of victory for the fourth year running. Most of his regular team were fine shots, while his son Archie and the Colonel were outstanding, and he smacked his lips in anticipation of the evening that awaited him.

The day dawned bright as the teams met outside the Lodge, where a fifty-bird sporting layout awaited them. The Colonel greeted his old school friend and comrade-in-arms warmly. 'Well, Pockle, do you think that you can beat us this year?'

'Every confidence, old fellow, every confidence' came the reply. 'In fact, in the interests of fair play, I thought we'd all use the same cartridges this year.' He indicated the slabs of ammunition stacked in the back of his keeper's Land Rover. 'Number six shot, standard game loads, not that small stuff that's only fit for breaking clays. Is that okay with you?'

The Colonel saw no problem with the idea so Lord Pockle nodded to Duncan Mackenzie, who started to hand out the cartridges, two boxes to each competitor. Willie, watching from one side, noticed the two of them grin conspiratorially at each other but took this for misplaced confidence.

As the shoot progressed Willie was alarmed to see how poorly his team was performing. His own Archie, normally the nemesis of any rabbit that was foolish enough to show its face within range, hit only six of the ten clays that were bowled across the grass in front of him. Even the Colonel failed to connect with some of the simplest overhead targets that were presented, and it became clear that this year's competition was going to be finely balanced. As Archie and Duncan faced the final stand the score between the two teams was neck and neck. Willie, now suspicious, went over to have a word with his son. 'Whit the hell's wrong wi' ye, boy?' he asked. 'Ye've no shot this bad since ye were a bairn.'

A puzzled Archie replied: 'I've no idea, Da. Must be oot o' sorts.'

Willie examined the ten cartridges left in the box. They were standard red cased loads bearing the name of a well-known manufacturer. He had a similar one in the pocket of his shooting coat. A thought occurred to him. Checking carefully that he was unobserved, he deftly exchanged it for one of those left in the box.

Duncan finished shooting – eight clays broken out of ten. Then Archie took his place; he only needed the same score for Glen Garron to win the competition and that should have been well within his capabilities. Sadly it was not to be. His first two shots missed the clays completely and he hit only six of the remainder, most of which were just chipped.

There was jubilation amongst the Inverpockle team. 'Drinks on you tonight!' Lord Pockle beamed at the Colonel, who smiled graciously.

'Bad luck, Wullie,' Duncan Mackenzie grinned at his neighbour. 'It was aboot time you got to pay for a round.'

Willie grunted and shook his opponent's hand. He was still puzzled by his team's poor showing. Out of sight behind his vehicle, he took the cartridge out of his pocket that he had removed from Archie's box and examined it carefully. There was something not quite right about the crimp. With a pocket knife he prised open the folded top, tipped the contents into his cupped hand and whistled softly. The cartridge contained not Number Six shot as the printing on its side suggested but something much, much larger – Number Three at least. No wonder his team had achieved so few hits; with so little lead in the air the odds were stacked against them from the start. 'The crafty wee beggars…' thought Willie. No wonder Duncan had taken it upon himself to hand out the boxes of ammunition personally.

He decided not to let the Colonel know of his discovery, but confided in an outraged Archie. The latter was thinking hard about how retribution was to be achieved as he drove up the road leading past his house to meet the beating team, while Willie saw their guests into the butts for the afternoon's grouse drive.

The afternoon went well. The regular beating team, assisted by the Colonel and Lady Mary, produced a decent number of late season birds and the shooting, while brief, was intense.

Willie oversaw the laying out of the bag. 'Twelve-and-a-half brace, no bad at all,' he announced. 'Make that thirteen,' said Lord Pockle triumphantly, 'my dog's found one that your pickers-up must have missed.' Sure enough, the elderly labrador appeared from the front of the butts bearing something in its mouth. Stopping in front of its master, the labrador performed a textbook delivery into Lord Pockle's outstretched hand. 'What the... ?'

There was a shocked silence among the assembled guns and beaters. Willie took the bird and examined it. 'Weel, that's no' what we wanted to see in the bag,' he finally said, in a grave voice. He held up the dead bird for all to see. It was a greyhen, a female black grouse, a species so scarce that both Glen Garron and Inverpockle were trying to encourage it into higher numbers by mutual agreement. Whilst an inexperienced gun might conceivably mistake one in flight for a red grouse, to such a team of guns the thought of making the error was unthinkable. To shoot one was considered a cardinal sin on both estates and heavy fines were exacted for the offence. Unsurprisingly, not one of the Inverpockle guns put his hand up to admit responsibility.

Willie muttered quietly to the Colonel who broke the silence. 'I think,' he announced, 'that given the circumstances, all bets are off. In fact,' he turned to a red-faced Lord Pockle, 'perhaps your guns might care to make amends by picking up the tab tonight?' A silent nod signalled assent.

As is the way of such things, the incident was deliberately not mentioned again and the party retired to the Kelpie for the evening meal and festivities. High spirits were quickly restored, though Willie noticed Duncan looking sideways at him on more than one occasion. As he went to the bar to get Amanda to top up his twelve-year-old Lagavulin, he bumped into Archie.

He raised his glass and smiled. '*Slàinte*' he saluted his son. 'I didnae even see ye drop that puir wee bird you found up by the plantings yesterday.'

Archie looked confused. 'But Da, I thought you'd done it? If not, it's still on top of the ferret hutch back at the house.'

'Nae son, it was gone when I looked in. I thought ye'd taken it – one of the cats must have had it awa'. Still, I canna believe that one of the Inverpockle lads would have been so stupid...'

Sitting with Lord Pockle and their wives in one corner of the bar, the Colonel noticed the exchange and the confused expressions and smiled quietly to himself. 'What's funny, darling?' Lady Mary asked him.

'Just a private joke,' he replied. Despite his advancing years, he was pleased that there was still not much that escaped him here in the Glen. He'd known Pockle for a long time, and although they were good friends he had no illusions as to the man's thoroughly elastic morals. The fellow had been so damn'd furtive coming out of the local gun shop a few weeks previously that he'd decided to make a few discreet enquiries of his own, with interesting results. Some things were better kept to himself.

He turned to Lord Pockle. 'This really is excellent whisky. I think I'll have another large shot – care to join me?'

FURTHER READING

There is a wealth of literature available to anyone interested in deer; here are a dozen personal recommendations for books that I find myself going back to time after time. Some may now be out of print but an Internet search should turn them up. As a starting point, a visit to Coch-y-Bonddu Books at www.anglebooks. com will usually bear fruit for both new and used books.

Alcock, Ian, *Deer – A Personal View* (Swan Hill Press 1996)
> A beautifully written appreciation of deer by a respected observer.

Almond, Richard, *Medieval Hunting* (Sutton Publishing 2003)
> A fascinating insight into the customs and practice of hunting during the Middle Ages.

British Deer Society, *Training Manual for Deer Stalkers* (BDS, regularly updated)
> As well as being essential reading for anyone attempting the Deer Stalking Certificate One, this handbook is a superb source of reference for any deer stalker.

Chapman, Norma, *Deer* (Whittet Books 1991)
> A comprehensive guide to the origins and habits of British deer.

Downing, Graham, *The Deer Stalking Handbook* (Quiller Publishing 2004)
> An excellent introduction to deer stalking.

Geist, Valerius, *Deer of the World* (Swan Hill Press 1999)
> A detailed and scholarly examination of deer evolution and behaviour.

Griffiths, Dominic, *Deer Management in the UK* (Quiller Publishing 2011)
> A guide to managing deer to their best potential from a highly knowledgeable and authoritative professional.

Parkes, Charlie and Thornley, John, *Deer: Law and Liabilities* (2nd Edition, Quiller Publishing 2008)

An essential guide to the law relating to deer and deer stalking. Every stalker should own a copy.

Prior, Richard, *Deer: Sporting Answers* (Quiller Publishing 2010)

One of a number of titles written by one of our acknowledged deer experts, this is a fascinating collection of the author's answers to readers' queries in his regular *Shooting Times* column.

Prior, Richard, *Trees & Deer* (Swan Hill Press 1994)

A comprehensive guide to tackling the problems deer pose in forest, field and garden.

Putman, R., *The Natural History of Deer* (Christopher Helm 1988)

A detailed overview of deer origins, behaviour and natural history by one of our foremost experts. Out of print but well worth searching for.

Whitehead, G.K., *The Whitehead Encyclopedia of Deer* (Swan Hill Press 1993)

An extensive and accessible work covering hunting, biology, history and a host of other aspects relating to deer, this is probably the ultimate in reference material for any deer aficionado. For a long time unavailable, but reprinted in 2008 by popular demand.

Revelation

Peruvian Tree Deer (page 175). There is no such animal as the Peruvian tree deer, I'm afraid. No deer are adapted to actually climb trees – and the vicuña is a herbivore closely related to camels and llamas.